COMPLETE
MOUNTAIN
BIKING MANUAL

COMPLETE
MOUNTAIN
BIKING MANUAL

Tim Brink

NH
NEW
HOLLAND

10/08.

NEW

Return items to **any** Swindon Library by closing
time on or before the date stamped. Only books
and Audio Books can be renewed - phone your
library or visit our website,
www.swindon.gov.uk/libraries

Copying recordings is illegal. All recorded items
are hired entirely at hirer's own risk

SWINDON
BOROUGH COUNCIL

First published in 2007 by New Holland Publishers Ltd
London • Cape Town • Sydney • Auckland
www.newhollandpublishers.com

Garfield House
86–88 Edgware Rd
London W2 2EA
United Kingdom

80 McKenzie St
Cape Town
8001
South Africa

14 Aquatic Drive
Frenchs Forest NSW
2086
Australia

218 Lake Rd
Northcote
Auckland
New Zealand

ISBN (HB) 978 1 84537 294 1

Senior Editor Sarah Goulding
Publishing Manager Clare Hubbard
Publishing Director Rosemary Wilkinson
Designer Neal Cobourne

Consultants Nicky Crowther and
Mel Allwood
Picture Research Steven Seaton
Production Marion Storz

Reproduction by Pica Digital Pte Ltd in Singapore
Printed in Times Offset (M) Sdn Bnd in Malaysia

1 3 5 7 9 10 8 6 4 2

CONTENTS

INTRODUCTION

What is mountain biking? Is it hurtling down a mountain at warp speed, jumping over logs and small children? Is it sitting on a remote headland looking out over the most beautiful vista you have ever seen, knowing that in half an hour you will find another spot that puts this one to shame? Is it splashing mud from a puddle into your riding buddy's face? Or is it fighting nausea on the final lap or the final day of one of the many competitive events the sport offers? In truth, mountain biking is all of these, and more.

Few sports offer as wide a range of options and activities as off-road cycling. Take a long-haired, tattooed bike mechanic, a pinstriped corporate lawyer and a bustling midwife, put them on their bikes in a muddy forest, and suddenly all three will be indistinguishable and will simply be fellow mountain bikers.

There are a number of reasons that the sport is such a leveller. It is a healthy, sensible, safe way of exercising. It is an escape from the noise, fumes and fear of cycling on the road. It is a way to explore new parts of where you live, and sometimes where you don't, and have a blast doing so. And it is an activity where riding with your buddies – even if they are only buddies for the duration of the day's ride – is more important than being the first back to the start. Many new mountain bikers who have crossed over from the road are surprised when you are happy to wait for them at the top of a steep climb, or after a whoop-inducing downhill that has scared them into walking – this time. What they don't realize is that mountain biking is not just about riding your bike; it is also about occasionally not riding it, just standing still for a moment and soaking up the sights and sounds of nature.

One of the beauties of mountain biking is that it is what you make of it, so if you want to race hell-for-leather across Africa in the Cape Epic, you can. It will take a lot more dedication and training than staying fit for a Saturday ride with your friends, but it is still possible for average riders to compete in the same events as the biggest names in the sport. Age-group racing makes it possible for riders from all walks of life to race each other on a level playing field, and this is true in almost all disciplines, whether you want to race downhill, observed trials or cross-country. It is only at Olympic level that the barrier to entry in events makes it possible for only the genetically gifted few to take part. For the rest of us, anything is possible with the correct amount of training, dedication, skills and equipment.

Which brings us to the *Complete Mountain Biking Manual*. This book is aimed at the already-hooked mountain biker who wants to take the sport to the next level, whether that level is simply being able to ride a favourite trail without putting a foot down, or ride all day without stopping. For many of the competitive aspects of the sport, the basics are the same, and focusing on them will not just make you a better racer, but a better biker too.

Whether you are looking at upping your skill levels, getting fitter than ever, entering and working towards a goal race or just looking for a technical hands-up from an equipment upgrade, we have it covered in these pages. And the more we can teach you, the more we hope to see other mountain bikers sharing our trails and enjoying our sport.

Tim Brink, 2006

WHAT IS MOUNTAIN BIKING?

In the late 70s, a band of renegades began taking their single-speed, drum-braked 'clunker' bikes into the canyons of California and riding them as fast as they could, wherever they could. The set-up was as far from today's lycra-clad mountain biking scene as it is possible to get, with the clothing of choice being a pair of cut-off jeans and a tight-fitting T-shirt with, occasionally, driving gloves that offered the only protection when falling off your machine. The most famous of these routes was known as the 'Repack Downhill', so called because it was so long and so steep that the build-up of heat from the drum brakes would melt all the grease in the hub, forcing the rider to repack it with grease for every run.

Gradually the bikes evolved and some of the pioneers – Gary Fisher, Charlie Kelly and others – started to fit derailleur gears to their machines so that they could climb to the top of these death-defying downhills without pushing their bikes the majority of the way. Gradually, triple chainsets, taken from touring bikes, were also fitted, increasing the range of gears to an impressive 15. Next was improved braking, and again touring bikes provided the answer in the form of cantilever-style rim brakes. Dedicated hand-built mountain bike frames first appeared in the late 70s, but the sport remained an underground phenomenon until 1981, when the Specialized Bicycle Corporation took the bold step of adding a mountain bike to their catalogue: the StumpJumper retailing at $750.

Sales were initially slow, but as people realized that this was an excellent way to explore the great outdoors, sales increased. As they increased, so did the number of organized events and races, and in turn more and more manufacturers followed Specialized's lead. Companies like Kuwahara and Diamondback were already established in the booming BMX scene, and the progression to full-size, geared bikes was inevitable. By the end of the 80s, mountain biking was quickly becoming a fully-fledged sport, with associations and events springing up all over the world.

1990 saw the crowning of the sport's first official World Champion, at the inaugural championships held in Durango, Colorado, after two years' successful growth of the sport through the World Cup series. An informal affair by today's standards, these championships were dominated by American riders, with Ned Overend and Juli Furtado taking the cross-country titles and Greg Herbold and Cindy Devine the downhill crowns.

The following year saw the beginning of the globalization of mountain biking, with the world championships moving to Livigno in Italy and the inaugural edition of the short-lived Tour de France VTT – a mountain bike version of the world's greatest road race. The world championships were once again an all-American affair, with John Tomac almost pulling off an incredible double by winning the cross-country title and finishing second in the downhill. Given today's almost exclusive levels of specialization at both ends of the sport, it is unlikely that this will ever be matched, but it does give us an idea of how small the sport was, and not so long ago.

The racing side of mountain biking continued to grow through the 90s and went transatlantic, with Henrik Djernis of Denmark winning three consecutive cross-country world championships. European domination also crept into the downhill scene, with the almost

Above: *Cross-country racing is one of the cornerstones of mountain biking.*

unbeatable Nicolas Vouilloz winning 10 world titles in 11 years, before retiring in 2002 at the ripe old age of 26. Thomas Frischknecht is arguably the greatest cross-country rider of this period, winning a silver medal in the inaugural world championships in 1990, and continuing to finish on the podium virtually every year until he moved to the marathon discipline in 2004, whereupon he finally won his first mountain bike world title. Towards the end of the 20th century, the paying public – in this case, television viewers in the United States – began to demand more extreme, more exciting viewing, and the X-Games phenomenon began to eat into the profitability of the sport. The age of big mountain bike teams, with full factory backup and huge salaries, quietly departed and mountain biking began to look back to its roots.

The sport evolves

When mountain biking first broke onto the world stage, the differences between the two major disciplines – downhill and cross-country – were so minor, both in equipment and attitude, that many riders did both. A set of knee-pads turned your cross-country bike into a mean downhiller, partly because the courses were designed with the bikes of the day in mind. Gradually, as suspension developed and downhill bikes evolved, the courses became more extreme and more difficult to compete on with anything other than a dedicated downhill rig – its weight and cushioning a hindrance to climbing. At the same time, the cross-country machine had become a fat-tyred road bike, with minimal suspension and just enough reliability to make it through a couple of hours of racing.

The down-side of this specialization was that the two disciplines had grown apart and developed their own, distinct cultures. Unfortunately, in many cases this was a separation that did not allow the two groups to interact, yet there is still a growing group of riders that don't fit into either the lean racing set or the lunatic downhill set. What grew to occupy this growing divide was called freeriding. This late-90s trend saw the development of lightweight, long-travel machines that could be ridden to the top of most trails and down all but the most technical downhills, bucking the trend of using ski-lifts or pickups to get to the top of a run because the bike was too heavy. Basically, the mountain biking market was crying out, in an age of over-specialization, for a bike that could be ridden anywhere, whether you wanted to race up a hill or down a mountain or even just get out for the day and explore. Freeriding in turn evolved into marathon and endurance riding and racing. These point-to-point races had been few and far between, and seldom longer than 40 km (25 miles). But as the sport has grown, more attention has been paid to training and fitness and the distances in these non-lap races have grown significantly. They are no longer two-hour sprint events, and it isn't uncommon to see winning times of four or more hours as the race distances have extended to a hundred or more kilometres (60-plus miles). The growth of these longer events has also spawned a growth of mountain bike stage races: multi-day events where the daily distances are longer than many single-day events, and often ridden in teams of two; and 24-hour events, a hybrid of lap-racing where super-fit soloists or well-co-ordinated teams of four ride a relay through the night and see how many laps they can cover.

Left: *Mountain bike racing in the 21st century: high-tech equipment and out-of-the-way places.*

LAND ACCESS

One of the biggest hurdles facing the further development of mountain biking is the rate at which parks and wilderness areas are being closed to bikers. This is not a new phenomenon. In 1964, US Congress passed a Wilderness Act that effectively banned bikes, and the battle between walkers, hikers, environmentalists and bikers has raged since. Generally, bikes do little damage to the trail if ridden responsibly. Skidding your tyre around every corner is sure to cause erosion, but in general most bikers know this and resist. The biggest gripe, however, is not the environmental impact, but the impact on other users of these open spaces. The perception is that mountain bikers are a danger to other people; that they ride recklessly down hills at high speed. While this is often a case of the entire sport carrying the blame for the actions of a few ill-disciplined riders, there are ways in which cyclists can regain trust.

Firstly, choose where you ride more carefully. If you are deciding between a ride in the local park on a sunny Sunday morning, with its dogs, children and picnickers, or a ride in a wilderness area outside town where you might see two people the whole day, the second option is the obvious one even if it is less convenient. Negative interactions with others not only give the sport a rough deal, they also ruin your day, so avoid them.

Above: Large groups of riders are generally only welcome on race days.

If you are on a busy trail – a legal one of course, illegal trail riding is never clever, no matter how unfair the ban – do not race around like you are winning world championships. Slow down when you see people and be polite. Acknowledge horses and their riders and pass them slowly, or even stop. If you do have an accident or a near-miss, stop and apologize and make sure everyone is okay before you go on.

The International Mountain Biking Association, an advocacy organization in the United States regarded as the leading authority on integrating mountain biking with other trail use, advises bikers to adhere to the following six codes of conduct to minimize their impact on the environment, and on other users:

Ride on open trails only
Respect trail and road closures (ask if not sure) to avoid possible trespass on private land.

Leave no trace
Respect the dirt beneath you and practise low-impact cycling. Even on open trails, you should not ride under conditions in which you will leave evidence of your passing. Wet and muddy trails are more vulnerable to damage. When the trail bed is soft, consider other riding options. This also means staying on existing trails and not creating new ones.

Control your bicycle
Inattention for even a second can cause disaster. Excessive speed can maim and threaten people – there is no excuse for it.

Always give way to other users
Make your approach known well in advance. A friendly greeting (or a bell) is considerate and works well.

Never scare animals
All animals are startled by an unannounced approach, a sudden movement or a loud noise. When passing horses, take special care.

Plan ahead
Know your equipment, your ability and the area in which you are riding and prepare accordingly. A well-executed trip is a satisfaction to you and not a burden or offence to others.

All-mountain riding

All-mountain riding is the essence of mountain biking. It encompasses the thrill, the freedom and the sense of being part of a wonderful planet. All-mountain riding is the continuation of mountain biking as it started, and revolves around just plain getting out on your bike and enjoying whatever form of the sport takes your fancy.

In its simplest form, mountain biking offers a fine opportunity to get some exercise and explore your surroundings. Cycling is an extremely healthy sport, in that it offers the rider the chance to get a great workout with minimal impact on the body. Regular running and walking both carry with them the risk of injury, from shin splints and stress fractures to iliotibial band injuries. The joy of the bike is that you can buy a brand new machine and, if it is set up properly for you, you can spend the rest of the day riding it without doing yourself any long-term damage. Try running a half-marathon when you have never run before, and you will almost certainly do yourself an injury.

One of the biggest benefits of mountain biking is the range you and your machine have. An all-day hike in the wilderness will carry a fit walker 15 or 20 km (9–12 miles). On your bike, you can cover that distance in an hour or so, and then go on and do more. You get to go to places that would otherwise only be accessible to multi-day hikers, you swim in streams that normally don't see bathers, you look back down valleys most people look up and wonder what the view is like from up there. It is a bit like being 12, on a summer holiday with your Raleigh Grifter and your best friend, exploring places you just know adults have never been to.

For all the idealism, however, there are some reality checks that need to be made before you can fully enjoy exploring your environment by bike. The first is your choice of equipment. The bike is relatively easy: fully rigid, hardtail

Above: *Mountain biking gives you access to more beauty than you ever thought possible.*

Right: Coastal trails can offer exceptionally fun riding and even better views, but take care on crumbling paths.

(front suspension only) or full-suspension, depending on your budget, will all do the job to varying degrees. For the average rider, a hardtail is the best bet, as a fully rigid bike will be awkward to handle on longer rides, and lead to greater fatigue. Full suspension is wonderful, but requires more regular maintenance and care, offers more that can go wrong out in the middle of nowhere, and is significantly more expensive than a hardtail bike of equivalent specification. A light frame with a medium-travel front suspension fork is usually the best option.

Clipless pedals are a must. Platform pedals and trainers will not only become brutally uncomfortable over a long ride, but are inefficient. The clipless pedal system attaches you to the pedal via a ski-binding type mechanism. The nose of the cleat on the bottom of your shoe hooks into the front of the pedal, and a spring-loaded backplate closes over the back of the cleat. Once you are clipped in, you can pull backwards and upwards through the pedal stroke, instead of just stomping down. Your feet are also secure in the pedals over bumpy terrain, and getting out of the pedals again is simply a matter of twisting your foot about 45 degrees outwards.

SOME ALL-MOUNTAIN RIDING NEVERS:

• Never ride a bike without wearing a helmet, even if you are just riding 10 m (30 ft) from the car to the trail-head.
• Never go on a ride without water in your bottle or hydration pack. You can't be sure you will find water where you are going.
• Never leave for a mountain bike ride without a thin jacket – the weather can turn nasty in a matter of hours.
• Never ride alone – and even if you are with people, tell your nearest and dearest where you are going, how long you can be and where to start looking if you don't come back.
• Never start a ride longer than an hour without food of some sort in your pocket/pack. An energy bar or a banana could be a life saver if you are out for longer than you thought and have run out of energy.
• Never ride without a pump and at least one spare tube – don't rely just on patches.
• Never ride without a puncture kit – and always ride with puncture sealant (such as Slime) or tyre liners, even if you don't expect thorns.
• Never ride in a group without at least one chain tool.
• Never ride without sunblock and water in summer, even on a cloudy day. Apart from sunburn, heat exhaustion is a real problem to deal with out on the trail.
• Never say never – some of the best trails start as innocuous-looking little paths.

Getting into racing

Mountain bike racing, in all its forms, offers participants the best of both worlds: a chance to be competitive and measure yourself against your peers, and a chance to be out in the open doing the sport you love. Just don't expect it to be easy! Cycling is one of the most energy-consuming sports around, second possibly to cross-country skiing for calories burned per hour. What this means is that you will have to work incredibly hard, for a very long time. All of which is good, because the thrill of the competition and the natural endorphin 'high' that exercising at a reasonable level offer, make racing mountain bikes a natural extension for most newcomers to the sport.

If you are looking at getting into racing, the first thing is to decide which side of the downhill/cross-country divide you are likely to fall. Downhill racing involves a lot of technical practice, a large amount of money for specialist equipment and clothing, and relatively little cardiovascular training compared to cross-country racing. If you stick with downhilling and become a contender at a reasonable level, you will need to put in some serious cardio training but, for

Left: *The exhilarating sport of downhill racing attracts the lunatic fringe, but is accessible to all. It is a great discipline for thrill-seekers.*

starters, this is the perfect discipline if you are short of time and love descending, jumping and are not afraid of regular tumbles.

Cross-country racing is more accessible as the cost-of-entry barrier to the sport is far lower. A decent bike, shoes, pedals and a helmet will get you to the starting line, and training, moderate bike handling skills and mental fortitude will get you to the finish line. Most cross-country races are held on a short lap – about 7 km (4 miles) in length – negotiated a number of times, so they are ideal events for introducing yourself to racing. You can choose to do only a few laps and, if you do bite off more than you can chew, you are never further than a couple of kilometres from the start/finish.

For the fitter and more experienced rider, endurance racing is a good option. Instead of going full tilt for two hours as is done in cross-country racing, endurance races tend to be single-lap events, ranging from 60 to 160 km (37–99 miles). The challenge is as mental as it is physical, as pacing yourself becomes more important than in the shorter events. And when you get it wrong in an endurance event, you are more than likely to be a long way from the start/finish area. Endurance events are popular with older riders, as experience, stamina and common sense can give them an advantage over the younger, stronger riders.

Above: *Typical cross country racers are lean and fast, such as Liam Killeen.*

Above: *Norwegian cross-country racer Gunn-Rita Dahle is a top female rider.*

A combination of these two disciplines is one of the fastest growing areas of the sport: 24-hour racing. Run on similar – and often the same – courses as cross-country races, the idea is for a team of four riders to ride in relays and accumulate as many laps as they can between midday and the following midday. Riders keep going through the night, using powerful lighting systems, and on some courses teams cover in excess of 500 km (310 miles). Then there is the solo category, which involves a 'team' of one rider seeing how many laps are possible. The top riders tend to ride non-stop, with Formula One-style pit stops to refuel, change into clean kit and get going again every few hours, but the more relaxed attitude is to ride for 12 or 13 hours, sleep for a few, and then ride the last six or seven.

Twenty-four hour races are a perfect introduction to mountain bike events. You get to ride the same course, often at the same time, as your top local riders, and you don't have to feel intimidated by them. Many teams do these events socially, with the whole team stopping for a bite to eat at lunch time, and often nobody lapping in the early hours as tired bodies get some sleep. There is no better place to learn race craft and bike skills from riders you would never normally get to ride with.

Above: Cross-country races start fast, and stay that way. They are the most physically demanding of all mountain bike races, despite the shortness of the course.

Cross-country racing

Cross-country racing is arguably the purest and most physically demanding of the mountain biking disciplines. Racing normally takes place on a short circuit, usually 6–7 km (3.7–4.2 miles) in length. At Olympic and world championship level, the top male riders will ride six or seven laps, and the winning time will be in the region of two and a half hours. Courses tend to be very tight and technical, with short, steep climbs rather than long ascents that allow the rider to build a rhythm, and sheer, twisting descents.

Cross-country races are generally used at regional, provincial, national and international championships, for a number of reasons. A lap course makes it simple to carry events for all ages and levels, without the need for laying out extra routes. If the top-level men are riding seven laps, you might find the women doing five, the juniors four, and the beginner and youngest categories only one or two laps. Because everybody rides the same route, it is a great arena for younger or less experienced riders to learn race craft. Generally, when the top men are racing, the rest of the riders from the other categories have a chance to watch how the experts tackle the technical parts.

Historically, cross-country racing has been a self-supportive category of racing: riders were not allowed any outside assistance, and so strict were these rules that riders have been disqualified for accepting a spare tube from a rival. The governing bodies of mountain biking have now relaxed the rules and introduced a pit system in which riders can visit service areas and get spare wheels and help with repairs, should they have a problem in a race. This was a well-received improvement to the rules, as it minimizes the cost of bad luck and mechanical failure.

So what is it like to race a cross-country event? The closest equivalent in road cycling is a time trial (ridden against the clock) – only here with a mass start. The start of a cross-country race is spectacular and frighteningly fast, as every rider in the field still believes that they have a chance at being the first into the narrower sections of the course. The penalty for being too far back at the start is that you spend the rest of the race picking your way past slower riders, and the tight, twisty nature of a cross-country course is not conducive to overtaking.

Once the first dash from the line is over, you will settle down into a pace that you think you can hold for the next two hours. Often, in fact, in most races, you will choose a pace that is too fast, but the nature of this type of racing is that, because of the high pace and relatively short distances involved, you will not have a chance to make up lost time later in the race, so you will have no choice but to keep going.

One of the keys to successful cross-country racing is to keep your pace constant and steady as far as you can. Smooth lines on the downhills, early shifting so that you are always in the right gear and don't waste energy hammering a short climb in the wrong one, and a steady approach to catching riders ahead will save you energy – energy that will be more than needed on the final lap.

Cross-country racing is great fun, and a fantastic way to get into mountain bike racing. You may not get to see as much in the way of pretty scenery as you would in an endurance event, but repeating laps and learning new, often better lines from riders, and then being able to try them the next time round, does your bike handling skills no end of good.

Above: *Riding in packs does happen off-road, but only in the first frantic miles of an event.*

Endurance (enduro) racing

Endurance racing is the best-supported area of mountain bike racing, largely because it takes riders through spectacular scenery, to places they often never knew existed, and because it calls on more than the brute force and course memory that makes lap racing so hard and fast.

There are two types of event covered by the mantle of endurance racing: marathon events and multi-day events. Marathon events range from 50 to 150 km (31–93 miles) in length, and are often a mixture of open gravel roads and technical forest or mountain riding. Marathon courses tend not to have the same short, sharp climbs and descents that their cross-country cousins do, mainly because the organizers have

so much more space to work with. To cross a mountain range and come back again in a 7 km (4 mile) lap is very difficult, but in a 100 km (62 mile) loop, it could be done twice. So the climbs tend to be longer and more gradual, requiring the riders to pace themselves and ride with some power in reserve.

Similarly, the descents tend to be longer and much faster. Top speeds on a cross-country race are unlikely to top 50 kph (32 mph), but in a marathon event where mountain passes designed for motorized traffic are often used, expect in excess of 80 kph (50 mph). And, unlike a cross-country course that you can ride lap after lap and perfect, every corner on a marathon course holds a potential surprise, so the pace tends to be a little more sedate and the intensity lower.

Above: Multi-stage races like the Cape Epic and Transrockies (shown here) take riders deep into the mountains.

Stage racing on mountain bikes was tried in the early 90s with a Tour de France VTT off-road event, but this never caught the imagination of the public and was short-lived. In the first years of the new millennium, stage racing made a big comeback, although with one major difference. The new generation events were not limited to the top professional riders, as in the Tour de France VTT, but were open to anybody who had the time, money and medical certificate to make the start line. What sealed the popularity of the majority of these events was the fact that they are raced in teams of two riders, with stiff time penalties for not riding together, culminating in disqualification for repeat offenders. This team format added a new dimension to racing, fostering teamwork and team spirit

Above: Many marathon events see riders pairing up in teams, and finishing together under all circumstances.

Left: Hike-a-bike (walking with your bike) is part and parcel of crossing mountain ranges. Here, racers competing in the Transalp must contend with snowy stretches on their way to the finish line.

only is there a long way to ride if you start hard and run out of energy early, but there are also many, many kilometres in which to catch and pass the early starters, once their engines have blown. Full-suspension bikes are a must for all but the top riders, as the longer courses will take their toll on your arms, legs, back and neck. This reduced fatigue level will translate into more power for the final stretches of the race, and better control over your bike.

Stage racing is basically back-to-back marathon racing, and the same tenets of self-control and pacing yourself apply, but even more importantly. Blow up in a marathon race and ride at a crawl for the final 10 km (6 miles), and you can have a drink in the pub and laugh about it that evening. In a stage event, you have to be on the starting line at 7 am the following morning, as recovered as possible. The keys are to race sensibly, and to eat and sleep as much as you can.

Both marathon and stage racing are perfect for the adventurous, and will suit older, wiser, more sensible riders. The distances may look intimidating, but with correct training, preparation and attitude, they are accessible to anyone.

both in the pairings and with other teams, while making the race safer from an organizer's perspective, as it made sure that every rider had at least one other keeping an eye on their whereabouts. The events are typically seven or eight days long, averaging 100–140 km (62–87 miles) per day, and with an average accumulated daily ascent of 2,500 m (8,200 ft) – just one stage would be considered a tough marathon event. The riders all pitch tents together after each stage in a huge campsite, and eat in mess tents,

sharing the day's ups and downs.

So what is it like to ride a marathon event? For some, generally fitter, less wise younger riders, the start is similar in intensity to a cross-country start. The more sensible option is to let the faster and possibly less experienced riders go at the pace they want at the start, and settle into your own rhythm. The winning time in races of this nature is often in excess of four hours, and the average rider can expect to spend more like five or six hours in the saddle, so not

Downhill racing

Downhill racing is perceived to be the simultaneously glamorous and dangerous territory of the mountain biking world. This is where you will find the tattooed, long-haired, rock star look-alikes and the devil-may-care, who-dares-wins attitudes. Having said that, it is a discipline where professionalism and respect for the dangers involved are of the utmost importance, as the consequences of complacency are huge.

A typical downhill course just doesn't exist, apart from all examples having a start point a lot higher than the finish point. Generally, the courses are 4 to 6 km (2.5–3.7 miles) long, and will be a mixture of the region's natural terrain and obstacles. In different parts of the world these obstacles differ greatly, from mossy rocks, to loose gravel, to near-vertical paths and jumps that hurl the riders metres into the air. What they do have in common is that riders are expected to ride, at high speed, on trails and paths that are near impossibly difficult for normal riders and their bikes to navigate, let alone walk through. It is testament to the skill and preparation of the riders, and the quality of the equipment, that this extreme end of the sport has proved to be nowhere near as lethal as it seems to spectators. In the 15 years the sport has had international status, there have been only a couple of fatalities in top competition.

Above: Downhill racing can often look suicidal, but the top riders, such as Missy Giove here, are always in control.

Getting into downhill racing on a local level is relatively simple: look for a local cycling club or organisation and get hold of a calendar of events. Once you have found some, spectate for a while so that you can learn some trail craft from the experienced riders, and then have a go yourself. The key is to practise each section of the course, each corner, each jump or rocky section, until you feel confident that you can get through it in one piece. Then start riding a couple of consecutive sections, lengthening your run until you can do the whole course in one go. Although the riders look like they are out of control when you watch them, the true greats of the sport rarely are. They have a clear line for every section and do not deviate from it.

So what is it like to take part in a downhill event? Although your final run will last between five and ten minutes, practising the course and fine-tuning your bike to it is a full-day affair, sometimes two days. The camaraderie at these events is unmatched, even by the team format of stage racing. Riders will share lines, knowledge and tips, knowing that there is no such thing as a perfect line and there is always a chance that somebody else can ride a particular stretch better.

Equipment preparation and pre-run routine are key. Before every run, double check every bolt and bracket on the bike, and your tyre pressure and suspension settings. If there are long pedalling sections, some riders will take an indoor trainer to the top of the course and warm up on it so that they are ready to race from the gun. Checking the schedules of ski-lifts or pickup rides to the start of the course is also important: it can sometimes take a long time to get to the start gate, and the last thing you want to do after two days of preparation and practice is miss your starting slot.

An offshoot of downhilling are the slalom, or fourcross, events

Above top: *Big air is a big crowd pleaser. Downhill races always incorporate jumps to keep spectators happy.*

Above bottom: *High speed jumping skills help riders to seemingly defy gravity with their impressive downhill tricks.*

that form part of most downhill weekend programmes. These events are run on an oversized BMX track, no more than a few hundred metres long and with plenty of jumps to please the crowd. Riders start in groups of four, with the first two qualifying for the next round.

Racing is tight and close, with riders tangling and crashing frequently, guaranteeing huge crowds.

Many downhill riders dabble in fourcross as a way of sharpening their bike skills and reactions, but it tends to be the former BMX riders who excel in this format.

Above: Tandem riding can be tough, but is almost always enjoyable.

Tandem riding

Tandem riding offroad is growing in numbers, but will always remain a tough branch of the sport to develop because of the limitations of the machine. The extra length and weight of a tandem limit it, in most cases, to more open courses, with the majority of cross-country courses too twisty and technical for safe passage, unless the riders are particularly brave and/or talented. This limitation aside, tandem riding is exceptionally good fun, and for a couple to be able to explore the countryside together on one bike may just revolutionize your partnership. The tandem is a great leveller, allowing a fit, strong rider and a novice to enjoy the same experiences and the same places in the same way. The biggest hurdle is really the cost of entry – a tandem that is strong enough to take the beating two people will give a single frame and wheelset needs to be very well engineered and built, and the exotic materials that make this possible, while keeping the weight down, are expensive.

Sizing is important on a tandem. The larger of the two riders should be on the front, as they need the strength and weight to control the machine. Make sure the front end of the bike is the right size for this person (also known as the captain) and then find the nearest suitable size for the stoker. The stem that attaches the stoker's bars should be adjustable so that you can customize their position. And the final word on tandems: fit a suspension seatpost to the rear as a matter of course – the captain sees the bumps coming and lifts off the seat in anticipation, whereas the stoker cannot see them and feels every pebble.

Singlespeeds

Singlespeed riders are the unconventional fringe of a sport that prides itself on being unconventional. The principle is to keep the bike as simple as mechanically possible by removing the derailleur gears and running a single chainring/single sprocket setup. This makes for a light and supremely reliable bike, but it is limited in that if you choose a gear that lets you climb steep hills, you will not be able to pedal on the downhills. If you want to pedal the downhills, you will walk many uphills. Singlespeeds do, however, help develop huge leg and upper body strength, and teach you to ride faster lines on the downhills, as you learn not to brake for fear of not being able to get up to speed again. Less niche than they once were, Gary Fisher, Salsa and Bianchi now all make off-the-shelf singlespeeds, as more and more riders decide to adopt them as an ultra simple winter bike to help save their precious full-suspensions for the summer.

Trials

Observed trials riding is as old as mountain biking itself, and is always a popular sideshow at major championships and shows. The bikes are minimalist, with a single one-to-one gear ratio, no seat to speak of, and smaller wheels. The riders are given obstacles and routes to ride over and are penalized each time they touch the ground. The obstacles range from rocks and logs to packing crates and even cars, and watching a good rider is fascinating as they seem to defy gravity. The best way to get involved is to contact your local cycling club or organization and ask them for details of local trials in which you can compete.

Left: *The bikes used in observed trials are very different to those used in other mountain biking disciplines. They have simple gear systems, small wheels and a rudimentary seat.*

Above: *Observed trials riding sometimes seems to belong in the circus, as riders pull off manoeuvers that beggar belief. Balance and confidence are key skills, as is a head for heights.*

CHOOSING A BIKE

The range of mountain bikes available can be quite daunting, but there are ways to cut through the clutter and find the machine that is best suited to your needs. The first step is to find a bicycle retailer that will be able to look after all your cycling needs. Pick one that has a combination of knowledgeable staff, convenient location, a well-respected repair facility and a realistic pricing policy. Knowledgeable staff can take many forms, often depending on the sort of riding you are intending to do. Look for a retailer that has a good mix of employees, starting with a slightly older and possibly wiser owner or manager, who will be able to help you keep reined in on the aspirations his keener, younger, more adventurous assistants may have for your riding future. It is important to listen to and feed off the experiences of the local dirt-jump hero and the regional cross-country racing champion, but use them as part of a bigger picture, one that involves you buying a bike that suits you and your needs, not theirs.

Keep it local

Finding a reliable local bike shop has many advantages. The most obvious is the time it will save you – time that is better spent out on the trail, maximizing your investment. But a more vital reason for keeping it local is that bike shops are natural hives of information on local trails, land access and events. You will be able to glean this not just from the management and staff of the shop, but also from other customers. Often, a shop will organize out-rides from its premises and these are perfect for meeting other mountain bikers and setting up your own network of riding buddies.

Mountain biking is a sport that is hard on equipment, and it is vital that you find a shop with an experienced workshop facility. Some bike shops include a free one-month service with new bike sales. This obligation to service and keeping your custom is another reason to stay local. Make sure they are qualified to service your suspension, can straighten wheels properly and even check whether the mechanics ride. Ask around at mountain bike events to find out which shop has the best reputation, but make sure you make your choice on positive responses not negative ones. Even the best workshop in the world slips up occasionally.

Pricing is something on which most riders judge bike retailers,

yet it is often the least important part of the entire purchase. How often do we hear of people who will drive to a shop an hour away to buy an item, just to save five per cent on the final price? The amount of fuel used to get there and back undermines the 'bargain', especially when your local shop is well within its rights to tell you to get your new purchase assembled/fitted/repaired at the outfit you bought it from. This is also relevant when purchasing items on the internet – don't expect your local workshop to happily assemble a bike you have bought from another country. You may have saved a fair amount, but you have threatened their livelihood in the process.

The best outlook on pricing is a long term one: your local shop will not consciously try to rip you off. It really is not in their best interests to do so and lose you as a customer. They are, however,

trying to run a business, and if they do not stick to basic profit margins they will not survive. Support them at the prices they are charging, but feel free to tell them if you can get something cheaper elsewhere – maybe they can contact the importer and find out how that is possible. If the other outlet is happy to put bikes on to the market at ridiculous prices, don't expect them to be around in a year's time when something goes wrong with your machine. It will amaze you how quickly the money you 'saved' on the initial purchase is swallowed up in repair costs your local retailer would have covered at no charge.

Anatomy of a bike

The different parts of a mountain bike can sometimes sound like a foreign language. Learning this language is vital if you plan on becoming involved in mountain biking, so here is a guide to get you started.

Saddle

Seat post

Seat tube

Rim

Tyre

Cassette

Spokes

Dropout

Rear shock

Front derailleur

Crankset

Chain

Chain stay

Valve

Rear derailleur

Gear shifters

Stem top cap

Stem

Headset

Top tube

Suspension forks

Down tube

Crank arm

Pedals/cleats

Rotor

All-mountain bikes

It sounds strange to be talking about all-mountain mountain bikes, but such has been the growth of the sport in recent years that ongoing specialization has created a need for a machine that does everything well. Some may just call that a mountain bike, but for the sake of differentiation we will stick with all-mountain. These bikes will allow you to just about manage a proper downhill course, are almost light enough to race in short races and are perfect for exploring new trails. Generally, these bikes are the most balanced in the range, allowing riders to climb efficiently and descend safely, but without excelling at either.

The great strengths of all-mountain machines are comfort and reliability. They tend to have a slightly more relaxed geometry than racing machines, which puts the rider into a more comfortable position and requires less brute force to control over-sensitive steering. Frames and components also tend to be less cutting-edge than on the 'faster' bikes, and will stand up to more of a battering. Of course, it is possible to customize these bikes to a level where this is not the case, but always bear in mind how important reliability might become when you are a two-hour ride from the car and forced to walk because a prototype component decided to show you its weak point. Confine such experimentation to short-course

lap racing, where you are never more than a couple of minutes walk from the pits.

Suspension travel on these bikes will be middle of the range, probably extending to 100 mm on the front and 10–13 cm (4–5 in) on the rear of the full-suspension models. There is a growing number of longer-travel bikes appearing, but bear in mind that there are two penalties for carrying more travel: your bike will end up heavier,

Right: An all-mountain mountain bike offers a great deal of flexibility.

and pedalling forces causing the bike to bob will be more exaggerated. That is not to say that more travel is bad – if you do the majority of your riding in rocky areas over gnarled roots, where tearing down the downhills

is the reason you are out there and uphills are a necessary evil, then the compromise is worth it. In general, though, it is best to stick with a 100 mm/10 cm (4 in) combination.

Suspension design is also a consideration here, and again it is a case of compromise. You need to look for a system that offers big-bump performance, but without robbing you of precious energy as you pedal. One way of doing this is to buy a bike with a lockout lever, either for the front suspension, the rear or both. This will allow you to turn the bike into a fully rigid machine on the longer, smoother climbs, where you really notice the bobbing action of your pedal stroke.

Above: *A full suspension mountain bike will give all-day comfort and control.*

More efficiently, installing a blow-off valve rear or front shock can do this automatically. These relatively new innovations stay rigid on smaller impacts and when you pedal, but will be activated when you slam into something larger, and remain so until things have smoothed out. Take a number of different designs for test rides before you buy, as we all have different riding styles and needs.

Disk brakes are a sensible option on these machines, as the extra couple of hundred grams they add to the weight of your bike will be more than balanced out by the extra power that the hydraulic systems give. Also, with disk brakes a dented rim or buckled wheel no longer mean calling for a lift home as there is no fouling of brake calipers, so they add to the reliability and versatility of the bike.

Tyre choice is wide open here, and will depend on the type of terrain, the skill of the rider and the weather conditions. As a general rule, a larger-volume tyre – 5–6 cm (2–2.25 in) – with a generous allocation of high- and low-profile knobbles, will get most riders through most terrain, and as you learn more about the bike and your abilities you will be able to fine-tune your choice. The tyres supplied when you buy your bike will be fine, and by the time you have worn them out, you should have an idea of what to buy next.

Cross-country bikes

Cross-country racing is exactly the opposite of all-mountain riding – short, fast racing around a tight, twisting, 5–10 km (3–6 mile) lap, with differing age groups and abilities completing varying numbers of laps. A typical cross-country lap will run to about 7 km (4.3 miles), will feature one long hill that may extend to 1 km (0.6 miles) in length, lots of short, sharp climbs, one or two fast descents and plenty of twisty singletrack. Pure performance is demanded, and the efforts required see riders accelerating from a virtual standstill to maximum pace hundreds of times per lap, with no really long stretches over which to build into a comfortable rhythm.

The ideal bike for this kind of effort is as light as possible, as stiff as possible and incredibly twitchy, when compared with languid all-mountain bikes. Suspension travel is sacrificed – most riders run just 80 mm – for efficiency, and lock-out levers are standard as riders need to be able to muscle the bike up to top speed without the front of the bike pogo-ing up and down as they wrench on the bars. Short top tubes make for compact cockpits, and, combined with steeper angles and shorter travel, the handling on these bikes is decidedly fast. Comfort is not an issue, as cross-country races rarely last more than a couple of hours. Racers are more than happy to sacrifice short-term comfort for efficiency, and the majority of top riders still ride hardtails at World Cup, Olympic and World Championship level.

There is a growing move to short-travel full-suspension bikes in this category, and a number of duallies on the market offer 80 mm front shocks and 7.6 cm (3 in) rear suspension units. On certain courses, even the top riders are prepared to ride bikes that are a kilogram heavier and marginally less efficient, for the extra comfort and control even this minimal amount of travel gives. A number of manufacturers have managed to reduce the weight penalty by eliminating a rear pivot, using flexible titanium or carbon-fibre tubing in the chainstays to provide limited-travel bikes that remain light and nimble. However, these tend to be quite expensive, and their longevity is still questionable.

The choice between hardtail or dual boils down to how seriously you want to race, and how much training and conditioning you will get to do on your bike. If you are a national or international level racer, who can justify many hours

Above: Cross-country bikes are at the cutting edge of mountain bike design.

getting your body accustomed to the battering a hardtail dishes out, and for whom every split-second counts, then stick with a super-light hardtail. For the rest, the extra comfort and control, not to mention the versatility – you will be able to join your buddies on all-day rides and be fresh at the finish – point squarely at a full-suspension option.

Braking is an area still very much open to debate. The purists still prefer lightweight V-style brakes, which are actuated by cable and sufficiently powerful. The problem with these brakes is that they do require more effort to pull, which can put extra strain on the hands, arms and shoulders over longer rides. Hydraulic disk brakes use less energy for the same braking power, and have the added advantage of being less susceptible to mud and water, but they are a few hundred grams heavier. The sensible choice has to be the disks, but weight-conscious riders might be willing to sacrifice a modicum of late-race control to stick with the Vs.

Tyres will be chosen specifically for each different course, but generally, cross-country racers use semi-slick tyres with a small number of aggressive side knobs for hard cornering, and virtually none on the centre tread of the tyre. This is to reduce the rolling resistance in a discipline where speed is regarded as more important than comfort or control.

Top: Cross-country riders need very high levels of physical fitness in order to compete at the highest levels.

Bottom: More and more cross-country racers are opting for lightweight full suspension machines.

Enduro bikes

The enduro, or marathon, category of bikes has evolved thanks to the plethora of longer distance and multi-day events that have sprung up all over the world. They endeavour to combine short-circuit racing efficiency and all-day comfort, so that a four or five hour race can be finished as fast as possible, and as fresh as possible, so that the rider still has some strength to contest the final kilometres.

By its very nature, this is a bike of compromises. It tends to have more suspension travel than a cross-country race bike, but less than an all-mountain bike. Steeper angles than an all-mountain bike make for a machine that handles almost as quickly as a race bike, with a lower bottom bracket providing a lower centre of gravity and offering better high-speed cornering for the longer descents characteristic of this type of racing. A longer

Above: Multi-day endurance events such as the Cape Epic demand enormous physical fitness and reliable, durable bikes.

top tube gives the rider more room, with slightly higher bars giving relief to the lower back.

For the longer races, a hardtail is out of the question unless you are a full-time professional and have the luxury of many hours a day of training to get your body accustomed to many hours of pounding. Realistically, the majority of riders will opt for a more comfortable ride, with 10 cm (4 in) suspension travel at the rear, utilizing either blow-off valve technology or a lockout lever, and a 100 mm lockout fork. Look for a simple system that requires little maintenance.

Above: Enduro bikes offer medium-length suspension travel and reliable equipment.

Above: *Always invest in the best equipment you can afford if you intend to get involved in enduro racing.*

A single pivot means only one place for bearings or bushings to get clogged with mud or dust, or work loose. The more moving parts a suspension system contains, the more chance you have of catastrophe in a half day of racing. Also, if you are racing a multi-day event like the Transalp or the Cape Epic, a simpler system will be far easier to maintain each night, leaving you to focus your energies on recovering for the next day.

Another important consideration when looking at enduro bikes is component durability. Five hours of hard-core mountain biking can wreak havoc on even marginally sub-standard components, so it is imperative to spec an enduro bike with the best quality equipment you can afford. In this case, best may not be lightest: rather look for tried and tested options, with a reputation for strength and longevity.

Disk brakes are an absolute must as they will perform better on the longer downhills that this form of racing features. Extended periods of braking can cause braking surfaces to overheat, and if this surface is the rim you can end up with tyres separating from the rim or blowing out. Overheated disks cool quickly, unlike rims, and will be back to normal in time for your next descent. They are also less problematic through river crossings, rainy weather and muddy conditions, all of which can be experienced in one race.

Tyres will tend to be a mixture of cross-country and all-mountain – large knobbles on the front to make control at the end of a long day as uncomplicated as possible, and semi-slick on the back for lower rolling resistance, depending on the race course and weather conditions. Rain or particularly technical terrain may dictate a more aggressive tyre on the rear.

Downhill bikes

Downhill bikes are the heavyweight boxers of the bike world – oversized, awkward-looking and awe-inspiring. Watch a video of some of the sport's stars gliding through a rock garden you would not dream of walking through, before launching off a jump and landing 10 m (30 ft) later, and you cannot help but be impressed.

The good news is that it is not just rider skill – or bravado – that makes this riding possible. The bikes are at the cutting edge of the sport, with the technology from downhill filtering down to all other aspects of cycling. The top-end bikes are running 20 cm (8 in) or more of suspension travel, front and rear, with single chainsets upfront. Downhillers try to use ski-lifts and trucks to get to the top of their runs, and who can blame

them when the lightest machines still weigh as much as two cross-country bikes?

A number of manufacturers have followed Honda's lead in building internal front gear boxes, as the motorcycle giant did in 2003 for South African world champion Greg Minnaar's bike, in an attempt to move the centre of gravity of the bike forward and to reduce mechanical problems caused by troublesome derailleurs and chains. Giant brake disk rotors, as big as those on motorcycles, bomb-proof frame construction and fat tyres, often as wide as 7 cm (2.75 in), round out a bike that would not look out of place on a motocross shop sales floor. And at a price that will make you think

there is a motor too! Mountain biking's most extreme discipline is anything but cheap, and it is vital that you find a shop that specializes in downhill equipment before you purchase one. Taking an inferior machine back once a week to have it fixed will ruin the riding experience.

Trials bikes

Observed trials are possibly the most specialized bicycles in the whole mountain biking arena: small wheels, wide bars, platform pedals and no saddle.

Observed trials – also called foot-ups – run along the same lines as motorcycle trials riding: get through an impossibly difficult course, preferably laid out over slippery logs, moss-covered rocks, electricity sub-stations and more, all without any part of your body touching the ground. Riders

Above: *Downhill bikes are almost motocross bikes with human engines.*

Above: The high speeds and improbable terrain that are a feature of downhill riding demand tough equipment and nerves of steel.

achieve this by hopping and balancing and wrenching the bike across seemingly impossible spaces, so the choice of machine needs to focus on lightweight yet indestructible parts. 50 cm (20 in) wheels, a departure from the 'standard' 66 cm (26 in) mountain bike versions, offer better manoeuvrability. Wide bars give better leverage, and bash plates underneath the bike protect the tiny single chainring from damage. Riders tend to use a one-to-one gear ratio for extra leverage and control, and powerful disk brakes for ultimate braking control.

Trials bikes are only offered by a small number of mainstream manufacturers, whilst the majority of riders source their machines from niche frame builders. Finally, the bikes really don't have saddles. There just isn't a need for one when you are leaping off small buildings for sport.

Above: Observed trials bikes need to be lightweight for easy manoeuvrability, yet tough enough to withstand all that is asked of them.

Tandem bikes

Tandem riding is growing worldwide, and off-road versions are now widely available. The tricky part about mountain bike tandems is finding one strong enough that is still light enough to ride. Two people's weight on one machine puts an incredible amount of strain on everything, from chains to wheels to frames. The key is to find an oversize aluminium or titanium frame, then spec it with downhill-proof wheels and industrial-strength everything else. Unfortunately, none of this comes cheap. Although inexpensive mountain bike tandems are freely available, they are designed more as comfortable road vehicles that should never be ridden on anything worse than a well-graded gravel road.

A number of manufacturers offer front suspension (and one or two rear units) that is designed for tandems, and this will transform the experience, both from a control and comfort perspective. If you are going to go this route, standard suspension forks – even downhill-specific ones – are not necessarily strong enough to cope with the extra weight. Check the specs before you buy. If in doubt, contact the manufacturers directly for advice.

Disk brakes are vital: rim brakes will overheat very quickly slowing down two people, and a tyre coming off the rim is less manageable on a tandem than on a single bike. Equipment choice will make or break your enjoyment of riding your tandem off-road. Always err on the side of too strong, choosing fatter tyres, more spokes and lower gears than you think you will need. Going more slowly back to the car is better than walking.

Singlespeed bikes

A growing return to the roots of mountain biking, singlespeed machines have just one gear – generally 36 teeth on the front and 18 teeth on the back, or roughly halfway through the gears on a normal bike. They are difficult to

Above: Off-road tandem bikes are becoming increasingly widely available as they grow in popularity. Tandems are great fun and a good way to share your love of mountain biking with a good friend or partner.

Above: Singlespeed bikes offer simplicity and reliability in the extreme. Although they have their drawbacks, singlespeeders are light, manoeuvrable and will improve your mountain biking skills enormously.

get up hills, as the gear is normally too heavy, slow downhill as the gear is too light, and seem contrary to every technological advance made in mountain biking since Gary Fisher and friends put derailleur gears on their single-speed cruisers back in the 70s.

On the plus side, however, they are immense fun, light and agile, and singlespeed riders get more attention, albeit semi-derisory, than the cross-country geek on the latest carbon-fibre race bike. The whole idea is that, by keeping the bike as simple as possible, with little chance of things breaking or going wrong, the rider's skill becomes more important than the

bike he rides. And singlespeeds breed a different level of skill: they improve anticipation, energy management and teach riders to pick the best line instead of just bombing through and letting the suspension soak up the trouble.

Purists ride singlespeeds without any form of suspension, but the nature of the culture is that if you want a front shock, disk brakes, and any other modern accoutrement besides gears, you will still be welcome. Wide riser bars for better leverage, high-volume tyres to soak up the bumps and a sense of humour are some other key attributes of a 'standard' singlespeed set-up.

ACCESSORIES AND GEAR

Mountain bike clothing has changed dramatically since the sport's earliest days. Gone are the dusty denims and tatty T-shirts that first braved the Repack Downhill. Gone are the sneakers. Gone are the days of come-dressed-as-you-are mountain biking. And all for the better.

Above: *High-tech fabrics and artificial fibres have revolutionized mountain biking.*

Above: *Racing gear now utilizes the most up-to-date technology for a better ride.*

Above: *Mountain bike clothing in the 80s involved some eye-catching colours.*

Today, it is about high-tech fabrics and tailored shirts, and the array of clothing and accessories available grows more bewildering as the sport develops. Fortunately, the basics are still just that, and a sensible choice in the foundation of your cycling wardrobe, with one or two specialist items for your chosen niche, will suffice for all but the most fanatical mountain biker.

The first phase of development in mountain bike clothing saw road-racing clothing being used, almost unchanged and offering a similar range of colours. It was, after all, the late 80s, and luminescent greens, pinks and yellows were at that time stylish and modern.

Lycra shorts had just hit the mainstream road-racing market, replacing, thankfully, the scratchy woollen shorts that had been the staple for nearly a century. The padding in the shorts used to be made of genuine chamois leather, which meant drying them incorrectly could result in your next ride feeling like you were sitting on sandpaper. Increasingly, the newer padded inserts were being fashioned from fast-drying, synthetic materials, which were cheaper, more comfortable and far more durable.

The materials used for cycling jerseys were also changing, and cotton, Lycra and a host of other synthetic fabrics were all tried with varying degrees of success.

Gradually, the colours became more muted as the initial growth of the sport expanded beyond the racing scene and came to be associated with outdoor pursuits and being out in nature. More earthy colours, more relaxed designs, loose-fitting shirts and baggy shorts – the look and feel became more hiker than shaven-legged road-racing professional.

By the turn of the century, mountain biking had grown to such an extent that it was no longer possible to generalize about the sport and say that mountain bikers wore a certain style of clothing. The only real generalization was that the sport itself was more relaxed and more open-minded than its asphalt-confined sister, and this showed in differences visible in almost all formats including the racing end of the off-road spectrum. Mountain biking and its fashion are relaxed, calm and neutral, whereas it might be said that road-racing clothes still clearly owe a debt to the 80s.

Shorts

Shorts come in two distinct styles for mountain bikers: baggies or Lycra. Baggies are basically board shorts with an insert that is made of a breathable material and contain a padded section to cushion some of the bumps from your saddle. Look for a contoured padded insert rather than a flat piece of towelling material. It will cost you slightly more, but the difference in comfort will make it worth the added expense. The outers of the baggy shorts should have no raised seams in the crotch area – even with the padding, chafing can be a problem – and if they have pockets, make

Right: *Although they are tight-fitting, modern fabrics and improved technology mean that Lycra shirts wick the moisture away from your skin, keeping you cool and dry.*

Above: *Lycra bib shorts are not just for racers – you may find them more comfortable than baggies.*

sure they are zippered if you intend keeping hold of their contents.

Lightweight Lycra shorts are more likely to be used by the racing set, and are a leftover from road riding, where the flappy outers on baggy shorts would rob you of valuable seconds. As a mountain biker, this dedication to decreasing wind resistance is less important as the overall speeds are much slower, but snug Lycra shorts will be more comfortable and user-friendly than baggies – just snag a gaping rear pocket on the nose of the saddle once in a technical section and you will either be hooked on Lycra for

life, or never again forget to zip your pockets closed before you leave on your ride. Choose black Lycra if you can – coloured shorts look great in the parking lot the first time you ride them, but will get stained with mud very quickly. Black material also offers a perfect rag to wipe your hands on after punctures, broken chains and other mechanicals.

The main reason the majority of mountain bikers stick with baggies is vanity – they look less conspicuous and more casual when you hit the coffee stop or pub at the end of the ride. Which is fine –

mountain biking is here today almost exclusively because it lets its devotees do it their way.

Shirts

Modern moisture-wicking fabrics allow manufacturers to make tops that pull the sweat away from your body and trap it in an outer layer that forces it to evaporate, leaving you cool in the hottest of circumstances. In mountain biking, it is vital to use a moisture-management shirt like this, as off-road riders do not create their own cooling wind the way road riders do when riding at higher speeds. Even if you use a hydration pack, which doubles up as a small rucksack for the spares and tools you want to carry on your ride, it still makes sense to buy a shirt with rear pockets. It is nice not having to

stop and rummage for energy bars, and better to stick them in a pocket and retrieve them on the move. Some manufacturers also offer zippered pockets, a great idea for car keys and money when you are riding bumpy trails.

Gloves

Mountain bike gloves perform two functions: protection and grip. Look for a glove that fits snugly – short-finger gloves do the trick in most climates and terrains. The first thing you will do when you fall off a mountain bike is put your hand out to break your fall, so gloves are a vital part of your armoury.

Padding is important, so shop around and look for gel-filled pockets on the palms and at the base of your wrist. This is where the major nerves run through your

hand, and you may find your fingertips going numb after longer rides without sufficient protection.

Mountain bike gloves have a thicker, rougher palm than road versions, and this is again necessary because of the lower speeds and bumpier roads that you will encounter. Wet conditions also make gloves a must: once you have mud and water on bare hands it is difficult to find grip. Some manufacturers offer full-finger gloves, which are useful if you are riding though lots of undergrowth as they protect the back of your hands and fingers from bushes and trees.

Below: Full-finger gloves are the best choice for downhiller riders, protecting the knuckles from branches at high speed.

Below: Gloves come in many shapes and sizes, but all should provide adequate protection and grip.

Left: *Stiff, carbon-fibre soled shoes are specifically designed for clipless pedals. Velcro straps mean that you can adjust the closures as your feet swell and contract, but they may become clogged with debris.*

Pedals

Clipless pedals are a must for all mountain bikers, offering better control, security and efficiency than either platform or clip-and-strap pedals. They work along the lines of ski-bindings, with a hinged back plate allowing the user to clip in by engaging the front of the pedal and pushing downwards, and disengage with a simple twist of the foot. Beginner cyclists can find clipless pedals intimidating – the thought of being semi-permanently attached to the bike is scary if you are not used to it –-but that doesn't last long once you have perfected getting out of them, which only takes a couple of rides. The advantages far outweigh the initial fear factor, as you will

have far more control over your mountain bike if you are not in danger of bouncing off standard pedals. Add to this the extra pedalling efficiency of being able to pull backwards and upwards in the pedal stroke instead of just stamping on them, and the fact that you can now easily lift the back wheel over small obstacles like logs and kerbs, and clipless pedals make perfect sense.

Shoes

Clipless pedals require specific shoes, which carry the cleat that attaches them to the pedal. They will have a stiff sole for efficiency – the top racing shoes use carbon-fibre soles but you might want to use a plastic sole if you are going to

end up walking a lot. The sole is built up around the cleat so that it does not touch the ground when you walk, and usually has a deep tread pattern that will grip on steep climbs when you are reduced to pushing.

One of the first decisions you will have to make when buying shoes is whether you go for Velcro closures, laces or a mixture of the two. Laces offer a guaranteed closure that will not get hooked on bushes or clog with mud in extreme conditions, but you will need to stop and adjust them when your feet swell and contract as the temperature and your effort levels change. Velcro straps are generally found on more expensive shoes and allow you to adjust on the move, but are susceptible to clogging and catching on things.

Ventilation is important on mountain bike shoes, especially if you live or race regularly in a hot climate. Plenty of holes, including in the sole of the shoe, will allow air to flow over your feet. Unfortunately, it will do the same in winter, so a less airy pair of winter/wet-weather shoes might be a sensible additional purchase. Use them in combination with mountain bike booties (overshoes) and you can keep riding through any cold spell without numb toes possibly causing chilblains.

Finding a pair of shoes that fits is also important. Mountain bike shoes need to fit as snugly as possible, so that there is no movement when you begin to pull up in the pedal stroke. If you have wide feet, look for an American-made or designed brand, while riders with narrower feet will do better looking for some Italian-styled shoes. Too wide is almost as bad as too narrow in an off-road shoe, as your foot spreads out in the shoe and can cause discomfort.

A stiff sole is vital, for two reasons: the contact point with the pedal is very small, so a stiff sole will spread the load and hopefully not create a hotspot under the ball of your foot; and it also helps with power transfer, creating a more efficient pedal stroke and, ultimately, making you faster.

Socks

Cycling socks are different from walking or running socks in that they should have no padding in

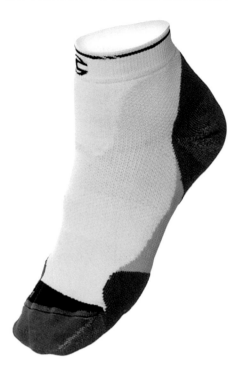

Above: *Ankle-length socks such as these are best for road racing, where picking up debris is not such a problem.*

Below: *If you prefer not to use clipless pedals, make sure the shoes you wear still have stiff soles.*

them at all. Road racing socks tend to be quite short, barely covering your ankle-bones, but for off-road use look for a slightly longer version. The gap that appears around the ankle-bone on these shorter socks is a trap for small stones, gravel and mud, and riding any distance with impediments like these in your socks is asking for blisters. Darker socks also make more sense – the road racer's white ones are a throwback to arcane legislation in the sport that forbade athletes at all levels of the sport from using any other colour. They look great at the end of a fit, tanned pair of legs, but not for long when mountain biking.

Helmets

Helmets are the seatbelts of the cycling world – no journey, no matter how short or seemingly safe, should be contemplated without one. The basic mountain biking helmet is a polystyrene shell with a number of air vents, all coated with a thin plastic that protects it from minor bumps and scrapes. What sets off-road helmets apart from the road variety is a peak on the front to keep the sun, rain, twigs and bugs out of your eyes. This will catch the wind awkwardly at higher road-bike speeds, but is a vital tool in off-road riding, where you will be riding in differing light conditions and on trails that weave through trees and foliage.

Your helmet needs to be as snug as possible so that it doesn't shift on impact. Setting the length of the straps in front of a mirror will take a while, but once they are set you shouldn't need to adjust them again.

Try to get the helmet to fit horizontally – the most common mistake is having it tilting backwards, exposing the vulnerable temple area. More expensive helmets have an adjuster at the rear that perfects the fit for your individual head shape and size.

Cycling helmets, like motorcycle helmets, are 'one-crash' items. If you fall and land on the helmet, its job is to collapse so that your head doesn't. Once it has done that, it cannot do it again, and crashing it a second time could be just as dangerous as not wearing one at all. Buy a reputable brand and have your dealer check a crashed helmet out if you are unsure.

Eyewear

Mountain biking takes place in many different light conditions, as you move from daylight to shade, from cloud to sunlight or from rain to shine. Your eyes also need

Left: Look for a helmet with vents to provide air-flow and a peak to protect your eyes.

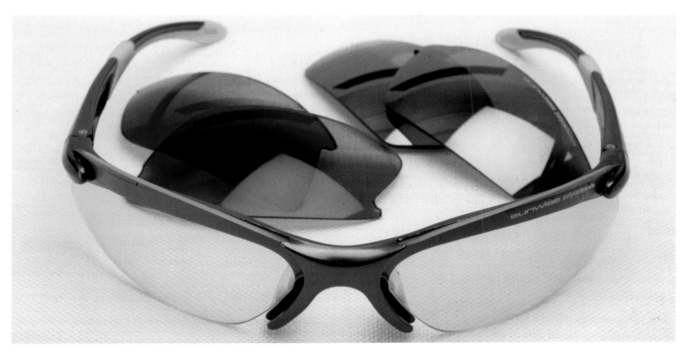

Above: Sunglasses with interchangeable lenses are a great investment for cycling.

protection from high-speed collisions with insects and branches. This requires a wider choice of eyewear than you would use on the road, where glare is your only concern. Look for a set with interchangeable dark, light-intensifying and clear lenses. The clear lens is one of the most useful, as it offers protection from dust and bugs, etc., even if there is not much sunlight around.

Fit and design are also important in off-road eyewear. A wraparound style is ideal in that it offers the greatest level of protection from flying debris. You also want a set of eyewear that will not fog up at low speed, when there is little airflow over the glasses, and to this end a number of manufacturers now produce ventilated lenses.

Sweat dripping into your eyes is not just unpleasant, it can be dangerous. If you live in a hot, climate where sweat is a problem, consider purchasing eyewear with a built-in brow pad, which will absorb and deflect the sweat down the side of your face. Alternatively, invest in a decent, thin sweatband that will absorb the sweat before it can get to your eyes.

Bar ends

Bar ends bolt on to the outer ends of the handlebars and perform two functions: they provide extra power on the climbs, and they offer extra positions for your hands on longer rides, helping to avoid numbness and fatigue. They range from short and stubby to long and curvy, each with its own ideal application. One

Above: This rider grips his bar ends for extra power on a long climb.

caveat with bar ends: if you have carbon-fibre bars, only buy bar ends specifically designed for them, with an insert that will stop the bars being crushed when you tighten the ends on.

Above: This hydration pack is worn around the waist and holds a 'bladder' of liquid. The blue tube connects the bladder with the bite valve (see inset), which is operated with your teeth. The tube can be fastened to your top with the clips provided, ensuring hands-free hydration.

Hydration pack

This is a small rucksack or waist bag that holds, primarily, a bladder that you fill with water or energy drink. A tube feeds out of the base of the bladder, and has a bite valve on the end of it, which you put in your mouth and squeeze open with your teeth when you want to drink. This system is a better option than bike-mounted water bottles, as bottles tend to bounce out of even the best of cages on rough terrain. The bladders range in size from half a litre to 3 litres (about 2–5 pints), so you have the potential to ride for four or more hours without having to stop and refill if you are using a large bladder. But the best thing about a hydration pack is that you can drink on the fly without having to take your hands off the bars for longer than it takes to pop the bite valve into your mouth. Do buy a well-known brand, though. The price difference is easily made up in the quality of the bite valve: the cheaper versions tend to leak, normally on you, leaving you sticky and thirsty.

If you use energy drink in your hydration pack, it is vital that you rinse it and the feeder tube after every ride. Bacteria thrive in warm, sticky places such as hydration pack bladders – the last thing you need is a stomach bug from your own drink source.

The hydration pack itself can also have pockets, pump clips and other storage areas for tools, rain jackets and food. All these fit better on your back than rattling around in a saddlebag, and since you already have a bag holding your water, you will not even notice the extra weight. Just be careful of over-filling it. Every item you pack in has to be carried for the duration of the ride. A waist strap will help keep your hydration pack from bouncing around on bumpy terrain, as will a chest strap.

Air retention

Never begin a ride without a pump and at least one spare tube per person. Most experienced riders carry two tubes – if you ride through a patch of thorns, you are more than likely going to puncture both wheels. Sealant-filled tubes are a must if you live in an area that has thorns; Slime (the top brand) repairs small holes as you ride, with the tyre only losing a tiny amount of air in the process. Some would recommend thick, nylon (known as Kevlar) tyre liners, which form a barrier between the tyre and the tube, but Slime is a better option and far less fiddly to work with.

Many modern bikes come with tubeless tyres. These help to avoid pinch-flats, caused when an under-inflated tube and tyre get squashed between a rock and the wheel rim, but you still need to

Above: *If you have a dual suspension bike with a rear shock system, always take a shock pump with you on long rides. It will keep your suspension perfectly set up all day, and if you suffer a unit failure without one, it will be a long walk back to the car.*

carry a spare tube just in case you get a puncture bigger than the sealant can cope with. Also take a patch kit with you, with some larger, thicker patches for repairing the tyre itself should you cut the sidewall on a rock or branch. Tyre levers also need a permanent place in your ride kit: even the loosest fitting tyre can be difficult to remove without them if your hands are wet or sweaty. Only use plastic levers on aluminium rims; steel ones will ruin the rim.

Tools

A multi-tool is a must, as is a chain breaker. Look for something

compact and lightweight, but with enough leverage that you can actually tighten and loosen bolts. Give your bike a once-over and see what you are likely to need out on the trail - the standard would be a tool with 2.5, 3, 4, 5 and 6 mm Allen keys, and both crosshead/star and flat screwdrivers. Only carry a chain tool that works with the newer chains, and look at carrying some sort of Power Link, a single connecting link with slotted pins, that allows you to join a chain without needing a tool. If you are riding a dual suspension bike, a shock pump is a must for long days in the saddle.

Essentials for marathons and all-mountain riding

Helmet Longer rides and early start times are the norm for both marathon racing and all-mountain riding, so a peaked helmet is a good option to keep the sun out of your eyes. Ventilation is key in hot climates – look not only for lots of ventilation, but also for sensibly designed ducts that will draw air on to your head in a wide-spread pattern. The lightest helmet you can afford – so long as it adheres to the essential safety standards – will also make a huge difference to your long-term comfort on the bike. If you are riding for five or six hours, an extra 100 grams on top of your head can be, literally, a pain in the neck.

Eyewear Dark lenses with some light-intensification will keep muck out of your eyes and cope with both bright sunlight and shade.

Above: A peaked helmet protects the eyes, and good ventilation is a must.

Most manufacturers make a yellow or orange lens with a metallic anti-glare coating, which does a great job of giving you the best of both worlds. A small packet of disposable tissues will help you to keep them relatively clean throughout the day. Wraparound glasses are ideal as they give you a wider field of vision and stay securely on your head.

Air CO_2 bombs are a good choice, but carry a pump and patch kit as well – you never know how far from civilization you might find yourself with multiple flats. A multi-tool and chainbreaker are also a must. If you are riding a new bike and want to explore different possibilities in the set-up of your suspension, or are looking at a ride traversing vastly different terrains, carry a shock pump. You only need one in the group, but it will help avoid a long walk back to the car when a suspension unit loses pressure.

Shirt and shorts Lycra shorts or bibs are a must for marathon racing, where you are locked in the same pedalling position all day, but baggies are feasible for all-mountain riding as you tend to be on and off the bike more. A

Above: Baggy shorts are fine for all-mountain riding.

pocketed racing jersey, even though you will probably carry a hydration pack, will allow you to have energy sachets and bars at your fingertips without having to stop.

Bar ends Longer, curved bar ends will offer you a variety of different hand positions, so you will be able to avoid numb hands and fingers on longer rides. They also give you some added power on any short climbs.

Shoes Avoid carbon soles – they are too stiff to walk in and you might end up with aches and strains if you are forced to push the bike for extended periods – as happens in both disciplines.

There are a number of shoes on the market with specially designed carbon soles that offer a small amount of flex to help with this problem, but they tend to be very expensive. A plastic-soled shoe will be as comfortable, marginally heavier and kinder to your feet and legs.

Gloves Short-finger gloves with lots of palm padding and grippy palms will help stop numbness, and keep you in control. Gel-filled pads are ideal, but can be a bit bulky. They will also reduce the amount of feedback you get from the front wheel, so if you are a speed demon on the downhills, you might want to sacrifice a bit of comfort for extra control. If you are riding in an area with lots of bushes and low tree branches, long-finger gloves will protect your knuckles.

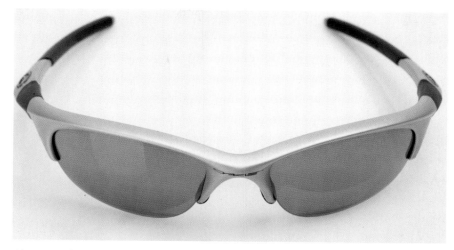

Above: Darker lenses allow you to ride in both sun and shade in comfort.

Above: Short-finger gloves with plenty of palm padding and curved bar ends will help to avoid numbness in your fingers and hands.

Essentials for cross-country racing

Helmet In a pure race situation, when you are crouched over the bars and riding at top speed, a peak can interrupt your field of vision. Cross-country racing rarely takes place at sunrise or sunset, meaning you shouldn't have a brightness problem, so a road-style helmet will be fine for cross-country racing. Ventilation is critical – this flat-out form of racing generates far more body heat than the more laid-back outlook in a longer event, and keeping a cool head – literally – will make you more efficient and faster. Look for something light and with a large number of well-directed ventilation holes that direct cooling air to most of your head.

Eyewear Clear or light-intensifying wraparound glasses will keep debris out of your eyes. Look for models that won't fog up easily, and possibly with a brow pad to keep the sweat out of your eyes.

Air Carry CO$_2$ bombs for instant inflation of your spare tube. They are expensive and can only be used once, but are the fastest way of inflating a tyre in the heat of a race. Most racers opt to not carry tools – once you have had a mechanical your race is over, and you are never too far from the start or finish line. At regional, provincial, national and international levels, racers are allowed assistance in designated

Above: Cross-country racers shouldn't have a peaked helmet to obscure their vision. Plenty of ventilation holes will make your race experience much more pleasant.

areas on the course – a change from the early days of racing where outside assistance was banned and just borrowing a spare tube to get to the finish was punishable by disqualification.

Shirt and shorts Lycra bib shorts will be the most comfortable and won't snag on the bike when you make the transition from riding to

running and back – cross-country course designers love to put one or two short, sharp, unrideable hills in the route to force a bit of portage, and the more efficiently you manage this transition, the faster you will be. Loose, baggy clothing is a no-no. A racing jersey with rear pockets, combined with waterbottles on the bike instead of

Above: Clothing for cross-country racing should not be loose or baggy – Lycra bib shorts and a racing jersey are ideal.

may need to buy dedicated bar ends with special plugs that prevent the bar from being crushed when you tighten them.

Shoes Ultra-efficient carbon soles for lightweight and rock-solid stiffness. The soles will not flex, no matter how hard you pedal, giving you the ultimate in pedalling efficiency and extra leverage on steep climbs. The only drawback of these ultra-stiff soles is that extended walking is uncomfortable and potentially damaging to knees and ankles, but in this racing you should be able to ride most of the course. Velcro closures allow rapid adjustment as your feet swell or contract in the race.

Ventilation is critical here too, especially if you are racing in a warm climate. Overheating feet are exceptionally painful and uncomfortable, and you will struggle to pedal at full power in this situation. Ventilation holes in the soles of the shoe and a light, well-aerated upper will help solve the problem before it starts. If the majority of your racing is in wet conditions, these well-ventilated shoes will also allow water to escape, so you don't end up riding with your feet in puddles.

Gloves Short-finger with little padding – you want maximum control and can sacrifice comfort in short races – and extra grip on the palms for muddy, wet and sweaty days. Some towelling on the top is good for mopping up the by-products of hard racing.

a hydration pack, will be fine for a short cross-country race, and your energy bars and sachets will be easily accessible for on-the-go nutrition.

Bar ends In cross-country racing bar ends have one purpose: extra power on the steep climbs. Because you will only be racing for relatively short periods of time – two hours is a long cross-country race – hand numbness is not really an issue, so you can install short, stubby bar ends. They will give you an extra boost on the steep stuff, but will not add too much weight to the bike. If you have carbon-fibre handlebars, just make sure that they and the bar ends you buy are compatible. You

Above: Good rubber handlebar grips should help you on the climbs. For extra power, short bar ends will give you a boost.

Essentials for downhill racing

Helmet Crashing a downhill bike normally involves a potentially lethal combination of high speed and trees or rocks. A full-face helmet offers the best protection, and relatively lightweight models are available from most manufacturers. They do not have a visor, like motorbike helmets, and offer little or no ventilation. Since most downhill events involve racing down a hill and getting a lift back to the top, the extra weight and heat shouldn't be an issue for most riders. A peak is vital in combination with the right eyewear, to keep the sun out of your eyes.

Eyewear Goggles with clear or yellow light-intensifying lenses will keep your eyes grit-free. Downhill courses tend to move in and out of wooded areas, and traverse such a wide and difficult variety of terrains, and at such high speed, that you can't afford to miss anything with glasses that are too dark. Normal eyewear can shift around on your face as you bump around, so a full goggle with an elasticated strap around the back of the helmet is ideal. It will also sit snugly on your face and keep dust and mud out, but do look for a ventilated model

Right: Downhill racers should wear a full-face helmet and goggles to protect them from high speed crashes and collisions with rocks and branches.

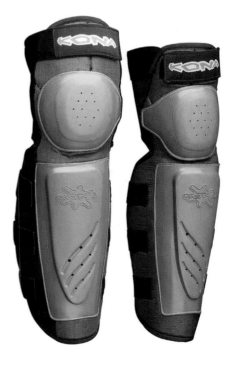

Above: Separate elbow-pads are a good investment, along with a body armour mini-suit to protect your spine.

that will not mist up when you sweat.

Air Downhillers don't often carry tools or pumps, as their runs are seldom longer than a few kilometres and their pit crew has all the necessary tools and spares waiting at the foot of the hill.

Shirt and shorts Baggy shorts are the norm, but more for style than function, as downhill races are so short that padding is virtually unnecessary. Most downhillers wear a long sleeve T-shirt as there is no need to carry energy food or spares, but make sure you buy one that is made of proper moisture-wicking material, as you will often spend time standing around at the start chute, waiting for your turn. The long sleeves help to protect

your arms from bushes and branches.

Body armour A mini-suit with a spine protector is a minimum requirement, and many riders opt for a more comprehensive one with a chest protector and shoulder and elbow padding too. Elbow-pads are available separately, and some riders opt for these, combined with knee-pads. Longer courses, especially ones with sections where you will need to pedal to maintain your momentum, might warrant not using knee-pads, as they can interfere with your pedalling stroke.

Shoes Many top riders still use non-clip-in pedals and fat BMX shoes, while others use racing shoes and platform clip-in pedals, or a combination. On really technical courses with loose stones and rocks it is vital to have a shoe with reinforced toecaps, as the front wheel can throw sizeable rocks up into your path. Many a downhill rider has suffered bruised and broken toes from snagging a foot or a pedal on a tree stump or a rock, and a robust shoe will help to prevent this. Also available are shoes that have a padded section for your ankle bone, and if you aren't using clipless pedals, you might appreciate this extra bit of protection. Personal preference will dictate your choice, but look for a comfortable, snug shoe that

will not pull off your foot in the extreme contortions that downhilling demands.

Gloves Long-finger gloves with plenty of grip are the choice for most downhillers. Because it is all about keeping as much control over your machine as you can, try to find gloves with little or no padding on the palm area. Padding will deaden the feedback through the forks, and at the speeds often reached in competition it is important to know exactly what is happening with the bits of your bike that are in contact with the ground. Reinforced knuckles will protect you from branches and bushes at high speed.

Above: Knee-pads are another useful item of protection for downhillers, but may interfere with your pedal stroke on the longer courses.

Above: A jacket with tight cuffs and an elasticated neck is essential kit when mountain biking in wet weather.

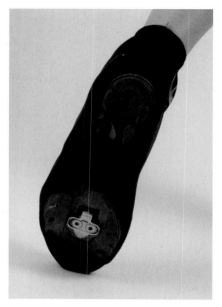

Above: Booties are ideal for wet weather riding. The hole in the sole allows your cleat to clip in without letting in water.

Special clothing for wet weather

Riding in the rain is a lot more fun than it sounds, and many experienced bikers will tell you that some of their best rides have been when the weather has been rotten. Generally, if it is raining it probably isn't particularly cold. However, even on days when it's raining but not particularly cold, as soon as you get wet and build up some speed on the bike, you will feel the chill. It is virtually impossible to stay dry on a bike, so the key is to minimize the amount of water that gets to you, and to keep warm.

Jacket Look for a contoured 'breathable' jacket with elasticated cuffs and a snug-fitting neck. The better the fit, the less it will flap in the wind, reducing your and your riding partners' irritation levels. There is no material that can realistically fulfill manufacturer's claims of letting your sweat out but not letting water in at full tilt on a long off-road climb, as the rate at which your body gives off hot,

moist air generally exceeds the rate at which it can escape the garment. Having said this, a breathable garment is still far better than a fully waterproof jacket that will see you wetter in than out.

Ventilation strips in the back and sides of the jacket will help stop you overheating, and most cycling-specific jackets come with reflective strips and piping, keeping you safe in the reduced visibility that attends rainy conditions – on the mountain this may not be critical, but mountain bike rides often cross public roadways and you will often need to ride with traffic to and from the trail head.

Some jackets offer a hood that folds away when you are not using it. Generally, you shouldn't need this, but if it is a bit chilly, it may not be a bad idea to have it over your head under your helmet. It will reduce your awareness of your surroundings as it covers your ears, so be ultra careful when you are on public roads.

Trousers Rain-resistant trousers need to be snug fitting so that they don't get caught in your chain, and so that they don't bunch up in the saddle area and cause discomfort. Most cyclists avoid wearing these garments, as they are restrictive and uncomfortable, and you can generally get by with a warm, semi-dry top and wet legs. If you are going to be riding in wet, muddy conditions, a pair of wet-weather bottoms will keep grime and grit out of your shorts – remember, the back wheel sprays water and mud into this area for the entire ride, and sand or grit between you and the saddle is a recipe for disaster.

Gloves Keep your hands warm with thin, water-resistant gloves. Cold hands can make riding very unpleasant, not to mention dangerous if you are struggling to operate the gears and brakes. Thin gloves can either be worn under your cycling gloves, if they don't have grippers on the palms, or over them if they do. Grip is critical in wet and muddy conditions, as your rubber handlebar grips will get quite slippery.

Shoes There is little that is more miserable than riding with your feet sloshing around in puddles in the bottom of your shoes, so wet weather requires a similar shoe choice to hot weather, except that the ventilation holes you rely on to keep your feet cool in the heat now serve as drainage holes. After you have ridden, remember to stuff your shoes with newspaper and put them somewhere warm to dry them properly – they can take a long time, and putting dry feet in wet shoes is deeply unpleasant.

Right: Full wet weather kit: breathable waterproof jacket, rain-resistant trousers with tight cuffs, gloves, booties and a mud guard.

Booties If it is cool and wet, or if you just can't stand having wet feet, a pair of thin, water-resistant booties will help keep your feet warm and your shoes clean. They will have a hole cut into the bottom of them to allow your cleat to clip into the pedal, and also a reinforced hole at the heel so that you can still walk a small distance without ruining the bootie. Make sure they fit snugly around the ankle so that water can't trickle into them.

Special clothing for hot weather

Hot weather is as challenging to prepare for as any other type of extreme weather, as there is less you can do to make yourself more comfortable. The obvious things that minimize exposure to the heat – stay in the shade, don't ride in the heat of the day – are not always possible in a race or multi-stage event situation, so it is important to do as much as you can to keep cool.

Hydration The best defence against the heat is proper hydration, so a large-volume hydration pack is key. Concentrate on drinking up to a litre every hour. Look for a hydration pack with insulation built into the bag, or find an insulated bladder, to keep your water cool. If you can't find either of these items, an easy and cost-effective workaround is to wrap the bladder in tin foil. It will not work as well as a dedicated insulated bladder, but it will help to keep your drink cool for longer.

Sunblock Essential in the heat, and not just because it will stop you getting sunburnt. By protecting your skin from burning, it is also keeping it cool. A waterproof blockout is the best bet, and carry a small tube with you so you can reapply regularly. Sweating removes sunblock faster than you can get it off by washing. Avoiding sunburn is especially important in a multi-day event, as the after-effects of sunburn and heatstroke can linger for days.

Head gear A bandana worn under your helmet soaks up sweat and will keep your head cool by not letting the sun shine through the ventilation holes, directly on to your head. Try to find a way to tie it so that the back of your neck is covered too.

Sweatbands are also useful for keeping the sweat out of your eyes. Modern sweatbands are far more advanced than the towelling offerings of the 80s. There is even a model that contains a mixture of tiny ceramic balls that wick the sweat away from your face and let it run down the straps of your helmet, not only keeping you cooler but also keeping the salty sweat out of your eyes.

Shirt It sounds strange, but a long-sleeve, lightweight shirt made of breathable material will keep you cooler than a vest. It allows sweat trapped in the fibres of the shirt to evaporate, cooling you down, and also keeps the sun off your arms. Another option is moisture-management arm warmers, which are as functional as long sleeves, but can be rolled up and put into your pocket if you tire of having long sleeves during the ride.

Left: Shorts and a vest top may the best option for women in hot weather. Make sure that they are made of breathable materials to keep you cool.

Left: *Although it sounds counter-intuitive, wearing long sleeves in hot weather can be a very smart move. It prevents you from getting sunburn and helps to evaporate sweat.*

Below: *Sunglasses with a metallic coating are the best choice in bright, sunny weather, as they minimize eye strain.*

Shoes Well-ventilated shoes are critical if you live, or will be riding regularly in a hot climate. Plenty of ventilation holes, both in the uppers and in the sole, will make your ride more pleasant. Also, Velcro-closures will make it easier to adjust the fit as your feet swell and shrink in the heat. Choose light-coloured shoes that will not absorb heat from the sun's rays. They will get dirtier more quickly, but overheating feet can be indescribably uncomfortable, and you will struggle to get power out of your legs if you can't pedal hard because the balls of your feet are burning up in the heat.

Eyewear Eyewear choice is also important in the heat. Generally, if it is hot it will be bright and sunny, so wraparound glasses with a metallic glare-reducing coating will minimize the strain on your eyes. A brow-pad will mop up whatever sweat is not caught by either the bandana or the sweatband. If you really struggle with sweat getting in your eyes, a light strip of Vaseline, just above your eyebrow and angling down to direct beads of sweat to the side of your face might help too.

Special clothing for cold weather

Of all the extreme weather conditions, dry, cold weather is the easiest to prepare for and manage, no matter how cold it gets. With the right choices in clothing and equipment, it is possible to cycle in temperatures many degrees below freezing, and the cool crisp air can be a pleasantly refreshing change from the artificial micro-climate created by central heating. The rule of thumb is that you should be slightly chilly at the start of your ride, as your body will warm up with the exercise.

Shirt The first priority in really cold weather is keeping your chest warm. The key to staying warm and healthy in extreme cold is dressing in layers. Start with a moisture-wicking undershirt, with either short or long sleeves, depending on what is comfortable for you. The next layer is created with a standard long-sleeve, moisture-wicking cycling shirt and then your choice of jacket as the outer layer. What this layer does is to wick the sweat away from your body, leaving it dry, and allowing the moisture to evaporate in the outer layers, instead of leaving a soggy layer touching your skin. Many riders use a standard cotton T-shirt as the innermost layer, but this defeats the object of layering, as it traps the moisture instead of releasing it, and cools you down rapidly.

Jacket The outer layer is the first defence against cold air, so if the

weather is cold and dry, a fleecy jacket should do the trick, with extra layers in the undershirt/cycling-jersey stage helping you to control your temperature. Wind chill – the drop in temperature caused by the speed of the wind – is an important factor on the bike, as your movement through the environment effectively lowers it,

Above: Cold, dry weather is easy to prepare for and, with the right equipment, can be a lot of fun. Layering is the key – always ensure that you are wearing several moisture-wicking tops and a good quality, breathable waterproof or fleecy jacket. Lycra tights are the best option for your legs, which won't feel the cold as much.

and the effective temperature you are riding in. Choose a high-tech fleece material that will keep as much cold air out as possible, or, if you are riding in sub-zero temperatures, you might need a wind-blocking rubberized jacket. It will not breathe much, so you will end up damp inside it, but you will still keep warm if you have got your layering right.

Gloves The next priority is your hands. Cold hands can make it a struggle to operate gear and brake levers, so keep them warm at all costs – even if this means bulking up your gloves. Fleece gloves will be fine in dry and mildly cold weather, but if it is wet or really cold, thin neoprene gloves will be required. These can feel bulky and uncomfortable compared to riding in thin summer gloves, but are vital if you want to keep maximum control over your bike in sub-zero temperatures. If your hands are getting cold, then, more than likely, so are your feet. Cold feet are not as inhibiting as cold hands, but can be very painful and uncomfortable. A pair of neoprene booties will keep them warm – just be sure to get ones with holes for the cleats and preferably at the heel so that you can walk.

Trousers Your legs will feel the cold less than the rest of your body, but it is important to keep them warm so that they can function properly. Cold muscles damage more easily, so minimize your chances of injury by wearing Lycra tights in cold

Above: You will still need a hydration pack in cold weather, but invest in one with an insulated pipe. This will stop the liquid freezing in low temperatures.

weather, with an option of fleece-lined ones if it is really chilly. Your knees are even more vulnerable in cold weather, with tendons and ligaments open to strain when they are not warmed up properly. To keep them warm, even in mild weather, wear knee warmers – you can always remove them if the temperature rises. If you are riding in sub-zero temperatures, a wind-blocking panel on your tights, covering the knee area, is a must.

Head gear Your head is an extremely efficient conduit for heat leaving your body, and will need special attention in cold weather. In temperatures approaching freezing, a fleecy ear warmer will keep your ears toasty, but as the

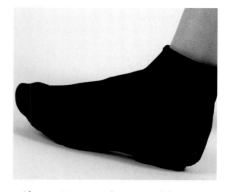

Above: Neoprene booties will keep your feet warm.

temperature drops further, the ventilation holes in your helmet will start to become a liability instead of an aid. A fleecy skullcap that covers the ears, or a full balaclava if it is seriously cold, will make your winter riding much more pleasant.

Above: *Heart-rate monitors consist of a chest band and a watch-like unit.*

Above: *When used in training, a heart-rate monitor can act as a guide. It will help you to judge whether you need to work harder or if you should ease off.*

Cycle computers

Measuring how far and fast you have ridden helps you to keep track of how much you are riding, and can also help you to work out how far you are from the end of a ride or a race. Look for a cordless unit that has a sensor on the fork, transmitting data to the unit on your bars rather than in a conventional way along an electrical wire. It may cost you marginally more, but there will be no wire to get caught in trees and bushes.

Setting up the wheel diameter is important if you are going to keep your distance and speed measurements accurate, and you will need to re-measure the circumference of your wheel whenever you buy new tyres. Different volume tyres will give you surprisingly large differences in circumference. The best way to measure this is to make a mark on the tyre and on the floor, line the two up and roll the wheel forward one revolution. Mark the floor where the tyre mark touches it again, and measure between the two. This will be more accurate than guessing from the computer manufacturer's specification sheet.

Pulse monitors

A heart-rate monitor is exceptionally useful in training, and good fun the rest of the time. At a basic level, it will tell you how fast your heart is beating, which gives you an indication of how hard you are riding. In training, this will not only let you make sure you are going hard enough, but also that you are not doing too much. It reads your heart rate from a chest strap, transmitted to a wrist- or bar-mounted watch-like unit.

More advanced models allow you to record and download data to your computer, retaining and allowing analysis of all the relevant information from your ride. The heart rate functions you can look back at include maximum and average pulse, while it will also give you your distance travelled, and at what average and maximum speeds.

Certain models also measure altitude and cumulated altitude gain, and when combined in the download to your computer, you will see a graph showing your speed, pulse and altitude at any moment on your ride. This is more than just a toy to compare your ride with that of your friends' – it is a valuable tool to track your training.

can increase its reliability so that it can produce 200 horsepower for extended periods of time, but unless you can increase the horsepower, all you can do is make it run to its limits for longer. To get faster, you need to increase the actual power output.

The vast majority of professional riders are using power meters as their training tool of choice, and while the price is still prohibitive – more than double an equivalent heart rate monitor – they are becoming more common and affordable. For the serious racer, power training is the way to go.

Above: *Advanced pulse monitors allow you to download information to your computer, meaning that you can analyze your performance in detail.*

The chest strap for your pulse monitor relies on moisture to pick up the tiny electric impulses your heart emits when it beats, so you might find that it does not pick up your heart rate at the beginning of a ride. Moisten the contact points before you put the strap on, and you shouldn't have a problem. Once you are riding and have started to sweat, connectivity will no longer be a problem.

Power meters

The next step up from the pulse monitor is the power meter. The most common version is a hub that replaces the one in your current wheel, and measures the number of watts you are pushing through the pedals at any given moment. Other options are an extremely expensive crankset-based version – that is touted as being more accurate and allows you to ride with different wheels – and one that measures how much your chain stretches as you pedal and gives you feedback through your heart rate monitor. The former is generally the domain of highly paid professional riders, whilst the latter is fiddly and difficult to set up, so your best bet is the hub-based system.

As a training tool, power is a more accurate way of measuring effort and improvement. As an analogy, you can tune a 200 horsepower car engine to run at 6,000 revs instead of 5,000, and you

Above: *Some models will measure your altitude and cumulated altitude gain.*

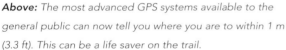

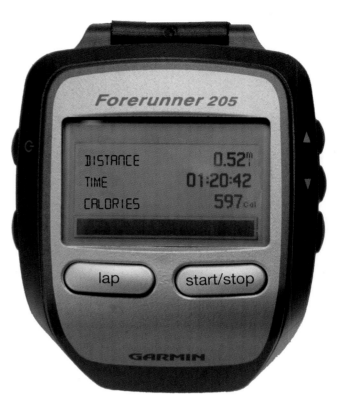

Above: *The most advanced GPS systems available to the general public can now tell you where you are to within 1 m (3.3 ft). This can be a life saver on the trail.*

Above: *You can keep track of your progress at all times by utilizing different functions on a handlebar-mounted GPS system. Here, distance, time and calories used are displayed.*

GPS

GPS is short for Global Positioning Satellite, but generally refers to a small unit that reads its position on the planet from this system of satellites. Originally developed for the United States military, early units were big and bulky, and had a margin of error of anything up to 50 m (164 ft) but some of today's units can tell you where you are to within 1 m (3.3 ft).

So why would you want to know this on a mountain bike? Well, think of it as a mini-map. First, it can tell you where you are on a normal map or, if you have local mapping software loaded, tell you where you are without the need of a paper map. Second, riding in the wilderness, or even just in a neighbourhood you are not familiar with, is made safer with the use of a GPS unit. It can get you back to where you started, exactly the way you came. It does this by storing waypoints every couple of seconds and, once you have decided you are lost, all you need to do is enable the back-track function on the unit, and it will tell you which way to walk, when to turn how far in which direction, and get you back safe and sound. Most units even tell you what time the sun rises and sets for your current location, so you can plan your ride to finish in the safety of daylight.

As the technology improves, GPS units are getting smaller and more functional and, when they combine speed, distance and altitude functions with a heart rate monitor, are fast becoming the ultimate mountain bike accessory. They do not need a wheel magnet or fork sensor to operate – although if you want the cadence function to work

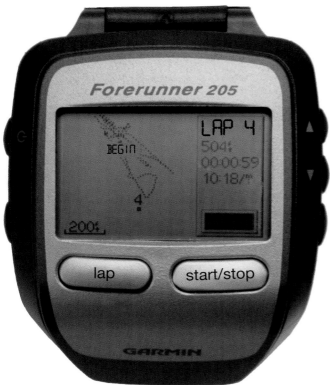

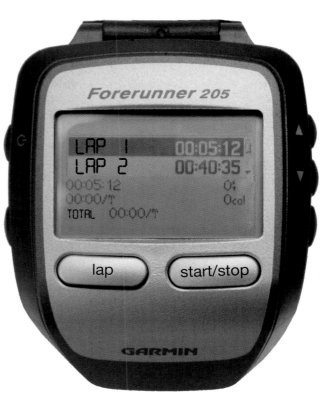

Above: *By creating a map of the route you have taken you can not only see how far you have travelled, but also how to get back to your starting point if lost.*

Above: *Keep tabs on your training by recording your lap times. Bike-specific units such as this have more useful functions than a dedicated GPS unit, but are still accurate enough for your uses.*

you will need a wireless sensor on the bike. Most hand-held units are supplied with a mount that lets you put them on your handlebar, and it is best that you do this rather than carry the unit in a pocket. The unit tends to want to have the screen horizontal, facing the sky and the satellites it gleans data from, and dropping it in your back pocket may give you reliability problems.

The best thing about these units, from a cycling perspective, is that you can swap them between bikes without having to recalibrate the wheelsize, as it is measuring distance travelled through your changes in position rather than how often your wheel goes round. And once you have finished your ride, you can even download the information and create a map of where you have been, and how quickly – or slowly – you got there.

There are a number of options when buying a GPS, but the choice for mountain bikers is to either get a cycling-specific one that does heart-rate readings on top of the standard functions the GPS provides, or a dedicated hand-held GPS unit. The latter will generally offer greater accuracy and store more waypoints, giving you a more detailed map of your ride and a greater chance of navigating your way across the frozen tundra but, for the majority of mountain bikers, the bike-specific unit will be sufficiently accurate. It will also probably be a bit lighter, as the manufacturers strip out some high-tech functionality to keep the weight to a minimum.

Women riders

As the sport of mountain biking has grown, so has the number of women taking part. The old-school way of getting the right bike and equipment for a woman was to get a small man's bike, put a shorter stem and a wide saddle on it and buy a pink cycling jersey. Fortunately, the market has matured, and women-specific cycling equipment, clothing and bikes are readily available. Shorter frames for shorter bodies, smaller bars and gloves for smaller hands, narrower shoes for narrower feet and tailored clothing together offer women all the cycling enjoyment and comfort available to men.

Shirts Many manufacturers offer a women's line with a narrower, more tapered cut and even integrated sports bras. Sizing can still be a problem, with some manufacturers creating small sizes that correspond with men's smalls, in an attempt to keep things uniform, while others have reclassified their sizing to create a whole new line for women. Look for a shirt that fits snugly, but is not going to cut in under your arms or around your chest. Many women opt for cut-off sleeves or sleeveless tops, thus avoiding the dreaded cycling tan, but it is better to have a proper sleeve on your shoulder for protection when you fall. Tan-lines are better managed with sunblock. Sleeveless vests can be quite uncomfortable if you are riding with a hydration pack, as the straps of the pack might overlap with the edges of the vest, causing chafing and irritation.

Shorts The most important part of any female mountain biker's wardrobe is not just good shorts, but the best money can buy. Look for a padded insert especially designed for women – it is a different shape to the men's versions. Speak to women at your local bike club and ask for advice

Above: *Padded inserts in your shorts and a gel saddle will make mountain biking much more comfortable.*

Above: *Helmets are available for women in smaller sizes and made from more lightweight material.*

on what shorts work for them, and once you have found a make and model that works for you, buy more than enough pairs to get you through a few years' riding, as you might find they are out of production when you need to buy more. The choice between baggy and normal Lycra shorts is a personal one, but the former are likely to be more comfortable and cooler.

Shoes Women's feet tend to be narrower than men's in the same size. A number of manufacturers offer dedicated women's shoes, which are slightly narrower than the male equivalent. The difference in comfort is marked. Riding in a man's shoe – unless you have particularly broad feet – will allow your foot to spread out, and you might find your feet getting prematurely tired and sore. Rather buy a shoe that is narrow enough and supports your foot properly.

Gloves Smaller gloves designed with slimmer hands in mind are readily available from most of the larger manufacturers.

Helmets The bigger helmet companies all have a line of small-fit, lightweight helmets specifically designed with female cyclists in mind – right down to a gap in the rear straps for a pony-tail.

Eyewear Narrower frames fit women's faces better than one-size-fits-all men's glasses, and the major makers all offer these smaller sizes.

Above: *Always buy women-specific equipment and clothing wherever possible. 'Making do' with men's gear should now be a thing of the past.*

FINDING THE RIGHT BIKE

Women differ from men in a number of ways when it comes to finding a bike that fits properly. Generally, most newcomers to the sport buy a man's bike of approximately the right size and hope it will do the job. When they start getting sore shoulders and arms because the top tube is too long for their shorter torsos, the saddle is slid forwards to compensate. Unfortunately, in compensation for the shortened torso, the average woman has much longer upper legs than most men, so they actually need the seat to slide a bit further back than their male counterparts to get maximum power. So now you are sitting hunched up over the bars, and you can't even pedal properly.

The solution is a bike that is specifically designed for women. A number of mainstream manufacturers now include models that boast shorter top tubes, slightly more relaxed seat angles, a better standover height and shorter, more upright stems that combine to produce a bike that is perfect for women cyclists. Not only will it be more comfortable to ride, but you will be able to generate more power thanks to being set back a bit over the bottom bracket, maximizing the leverage from a woman's longer femur.

The other advantage of having a bike specifically designed for the female body is that the shorter,

more upright position will put the rider in a better position on the saddle. Leaning too far forward can cause soft tissue damage in areas that will make it very difficult to sit on a saddle again in the near future.

Above: Top cross-country riders such as Gunn-Rita Dahle have proved that women can be just as successful as men in the arena of mountain biking.

Of all the purchases you will make for your bike, the saddle you choose will make the difference between a short first ride followed by no further rides, and a long and happy partnership with your bike. You want to be sitting on the bones of your pelvis, and the female pelvis is wider than the male's. Look for a model that is wider than a man's saddle, with a cut-out groove down the middle that minimizes soft tissue contact with the seat, and generous gel padding in the meat of the saddle. Titanium rails are marginally lighter than their steel or aluminium counterparts, helping keep the weight of the bike down, but have a more important role in that they flex and offer a modicum of shock absorption too. At first, any saddle will feel like a torture device to men and women alike, but with careful choice, as you body adapts to cycling, you will find a saddle that minimizes the battering this area takes.

Handlebars and grips A couple of big manufacturers offer smaller-diameter handlebars and grips, which are easier to grip for smaller hands. Before you buy a set, make sure that you can get hold of spares should you need them as they are not readily available yet. Also, adjust your brake levers so they sit closer to the bars. You will lose out on a bit of cable travel, so they will need to be set more precisely, but at least you will be able to reach them quickly.

Top: Choose your saddle carefully. Gel padding and a groove down the centre will make for a more comfortable ride.

Bottom: Some manufacturers now offer bikes with smaller handlebars and grips, designed for smaller hands.

MAINTENANCE AND REPAIR

Bike maintenance and repair is something that most people can manage, given the correct tools and a little knowledge. There are certain areas that are easier than others, but if you have the time to learn, and the time to actually spend tinkering in your garage, doing as much as you can yourself can be not only rewarding, but also cost-effective. Having said that, there is some comfort to be had in taking your bike into your local bike shop and getting it back a few days later, spotlessly clean and working like new.

Above: Your local bike shop will have the expertise for more advanced maintenance.

So what is realistically within the reach of the home-mechanic? Cleaning is the first, and arguably most important, thing you can do at home. A clean bike works considerably better than a dirty one, and it also stays working better for longer, as there is less grit and grime to foul in the chain and bearings.

Removing and replacing the chain and cables is also technically fairly simple, and can be done with a minimum of fuss at home. You may need to spend more time setting the indexing on the gears than the bike shop mechanic, but that is only because he does it so often that it is intuitive. Fixing punctures and changing tubes and tyres is standard fare for all cyclists and should also be handled at home. Repacking bearings and changing cassettes is fiddly, messy work, although still do-able at home by more advanced mechanics, but hydraulic brake systems, suspension forks and rear shocks are probably best left to the experts, unless you are particularly mechanically gifted.

Below is a range of the tools and equipment that you should have in your arsenal if you are going to attempt the basics of home repair. If you have the space, a pegboard is ideal for storage, otherwise a large toolbox with separate compartments for each set of items will do the job. Always buy the most expensive tool you can afford – cheap tools damage easily and can also damage your bike and equipment.

A repair stand will make a world of difference, letting you reach everything on the bike without having to crouch or leave it leaning against a wall while you bolt bits to it.

Below: A good range of tools including wrenches, spanners, Allen keys, screwdrivers, lubricant, spare chain, chain tool and a shock pump are essential for home repair.

Cleaning

Cleaning your bike properly should, ideally, be done after every significant ride and certainly every time you ride through mud, heavy dust or water. Cleaning is not just a cosmetic action, it also keeps your equipment working better, reduces wear and tear on areas like the chain, cassette, chainrings and brake blocks, and gives you the opportunity to check for cracks and other damage.

Start by hosing the bike down. If you are using a high-pressure hose, take extra care not to direct the spray straight into the hub, bottom bracket and headset bearings, as you could replace the grease with water and irreparably damage the bearing surfaces. Remove the wheels and hoist the bike into your repair stand. Apply degreaser to the chain, cassette and chainrings, and allow to stand for a few minutes, then scrub everything with your assortment of brushes and sponges, using hot, soapy water.

Once you have got every bit of grit out of every crevice on the bike, rinse everything with clean water, and wipe the lot down with a dry cloth. This is the ideal time to check every inch of the bike for cracks and damage, and to inspect the tyres for cuts and nicks.

The final action is to lubricate the chain and the pivot points, using a dry bike-specific lube. If you are going to be riding in very muddy conditions, you can apply a light coating of spray cooking oil to everything except the braking surfaces, the tyres and the grips – this will minimize the amount of mud that will stick to the bike, making it easier to clean when you get back from your next ride.

ESSENTIAL EQUIPMENT

- Bucket with hot, soapy water
- Degreaser
- Large stiff brush
- Small softer brush
- Sponges
- Cassette scraper
- Cloth

1 The easiest way to clean the bike is to hose it down, then put it in a repair stand, remove the wheels and put an old quick-release in the rear dropouts to keep the chain tension. This will help you to clean

Above: Make sure you have a good selection of different sized brushes.

it when you need to run it through a degreaser-filled sponge.

2 Pick all the large bits of grease from the cassette using the cassette scraper, then use a stiff brush and degreaser to clean thoroughly.

1 Before cleaning, put the bike on a repair stand and remove the wheels.

2 Use the cassette scraper to clean the worst of the grease and gunk off.

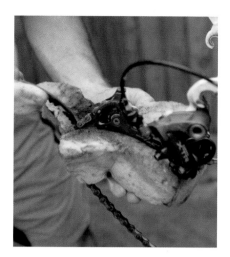

3a Scrub the whole bike thoroughly with hot, soapy water.

3 Spray degreaser onto the chain, chainrings and rear derailleur pulley wheels. Allow to stand for a few minutes and then scrub the entire bike with hot, soapy water, using sponges and brushes to reach awkward areas. Start from the top of the bike and work downwards, so that recently cleaned parts are not fouled.

4 Put the wheels back on the bike and rinse with clean water. Wipe as much as you can with a dry cloth and lube the chain and the pivot points of the derailleur (**5**).

4 Once the wheels are back on, rinse everything with clean water. Dry as much as you can to prevent rusting.

3b Use special brushes for awkward areas.

3c Start at the top and work downwards.

5 Remember to lubricate the moving parts to keep them in good working order.

Pre-ride safety check

Mountain biking, by its very nature, is incredibly hard on bikes and equipment. Before you ride, it is important to run through the following checklist. It may seem silly to do this every time, when you know full well that everything was fine when you last rode, but all it takes is one slipped brake cable, or a loose quick-release to ruin a ride.

1 Check for play in the wheel bearings by holding the bike still and moving the tyre laterally with your hand. Play indicates loose bearings or a broken axle, both of which require attention if you want to avoid permanent damage.

2 Check both wheel quick-releases and the seat quick-release, to see that they are tightened as they should be.

3 Check the headset for play by locking the front brake and rocking backwards and forwards. Put a hand on the top and then the bottom races and feel for play. This would need attention before you ride – it could either be from loose bearings or a cracked steerer tube.

4 Check your suspension fork for excess play by gripping the wheel between your knees and twisting the handlebars. Excess play here should be looked at by a suspension specialist.

5 Check that all stem bolts are tight, both at the handlebar and at the steerer tube.

6 Check the rear shock unit for leaking oil, which could be a sign that all is not well.

1 Hold the bike still and move the tyre to check for play.

2 Check the quick releases and make sure they are suitably tight.

3 Lock the brake and feel for any play in the headset that needs attention.

4 Grip the wheel between your knees and twist the handlebars to check the fork.

5 Make sure the stem bolts are tight, adjusting with an Allen key if necessary.

6 Leaking oil from the rear shock unit is not a good sign.

Weekly checklist

The majority of accidents caused by equipment failure could have been prevented had they been caught in time. And even if it is just to avoid walking back to your car when a component breaks, take the time, at least once a week, to check the following areas of your bike carefully. The perfect time to do this is when you are cleaning the bike.

1 Frayed or damaged cables can snap, causing you to lose braking power, or gear selection. Check the bolts that hold the cables too, and if you have hydraulic disk brakes, check the hydraulic hoses for signs of leaking.

2 Pull the brake levers and check that the cables are taut enough, or that there is no compromise in the hydraulic system. You shouldn't be able to get the lever to touch the handlebar.

3 Check the sidewalls of the tyres for cuts, and the main tread for wear, cuts and missing knobbles.

4 Holding the frame in one hand, grip the pedal and feel for play in the bottom bracket area.

5 Check the frame for cracks, in particular behind the head tube and around the bottom bracket area where cracks are most likely to form.

6 Check the area around the seat tube as well, where the seat post enters the frame. There is an enormous amount of leverage through this junction, and cracks may form.

1 Frayed cables should be replaced as soon as you notice them.

2 You should not be able to pull the brake lever all the way back to the handlebar.

3 Check the tyres carefully for cuts and general wear and tear.

4 Holding the pedal, make sure there is no play in the bottom bracket area.

5 Make sure there are no cracks around the head tube.

6 The area where the seat tube enters the frame is a prime place for cracks to form.

Bottom brackets

Servicing the bottom bracket should be done every three months, or more regularly if you ride through lots of mud or deep water. There are three basic types of bottom bracket: cartridge, open bearing and outboard bearing.

Cartridge bottom brackets are essentially throw-away units and once they show sign of wear, usually through movement in the cranks, just replace them with new ones. This is a relatively inexpensive exercise. If you are experiencing a creaking bottom bracket, remove it and clean and grease the threads both on the bottom bracket and the frame before replacing.

Open bearing bottom brackets are unusual today, with the vast majority of bikes using the cartridge type. If your bike is old enough to still have one of these, it is probably best to get a shop to repair and regrease it, as the final setup of the cones and bearings is quite fiddly. Or you could replace it with a cartridge if it is showing signs of wear.

Outboard bearing bottom brackets were developed for the mass market by Shimano early in the new millennium. The bearings sit proud of the frame, and the right-hand crank and bottom bracket axle are one unit, with the left-hand crank clamping onto the open end of the axle. This offers a wider base for the bearings, for stiffer, lighter cranks, and a more serviceable bottom bracket.

1 Using the correct tool, tighten the outer part of the tool into the crank threads.

2 Tighten the inner part of the tool in order to push the crank off the axle.

3 Use the dedicated tool to remove and replace the bottom bracket.

CARTRIDGE BOTTOM BRACKET REPLACEMENT

1 Remove both cranks and remove the left-hand cup, using the dedicated tool, by turning it anti-clockwise.
2 Using the same tool, remove the right-hand side of the bottom bracket by turning it clockwise.
3 After cleaning all dirt from all threads, apply a thin layer of grease and reverse the process to reinstall.

1 Remove both the crank arms.

2 The correct tool fits into the notches in the bottom bracket cups.

3 Apply grease before replacing and tightening the cups.

REGREASING BOTTOM BRACKET THREADS

1 Remove both crank arms, using either the correct tool or an 8 mm Allen key (see below).

2 Using a bottom bracket tool, remove the left hand cup by turning anti-clockwise, then the right-hand cup by turning clockwise.

3 Clean and grease the threads on the bottom bracket and inside the frame, then refit the bottom bracket. Tighten the right hand cup anti-clockwise, then the left hand cup clockwise. Refit the crank arms, then tighten crank bolts firmly.

REMOVING CRANK ARMS

1 Old-style square taper cranks will require a special crank-puller tool to remove the arms, once you have unscrewed the crank bolts.

2 More modern cranks have a self-extraction Allen key unit that simply requires an 8 mm Allen key to screw the crank on or off.

1 Square taper cranks require a special tool to remove them.

2 More modern cranks will just need an Allen key to disassemble.

Removing and replacing your chain

The chain is the heart of the bicycle, and after more than a century of development, is still the most energy-efficient way of getting legs to turn wheels. It is made up of a series of inner and outer links that crimp together around loose-fitting rollers with the help of short pins.

A clean chain will last longer and be more efficient, as the rollers wear with accumulated grime and grit, causing the chain to flex and slip. The best way to clean the chain is to remove it from the bike and soak it in degreaser, before rejoining it on the bike and lubricating it.

Worn chains should be replaced before they have a chance to wear your expensive cassette sprockets and chainrings. Check for wear either by using a dedicated tool, or by checking how tight the chain is around the largest chainring on the bike – you should only be able to lift it a couple of millimetres; more than that and it is time to replace it.

The latest chains have a specific pin that should only be used for breaking and rejoining the chain, and failure to do so could lead to a broken chain. It is generally a different colour and profile to the rest of the chain pins, but check the literature that came with the chain to be sure. Special tool-free links are currently gaining in popularity, and make removing,

cleaning and replacing the chain exceptionally simple.

1 The first job is to cut the new chain to the correct length. With the chain in the biggest chainring and the smallest rear sprocket, the rear derailleur jockey wheels should be directly above each other. Cut the relevant number of pairs of links you need to remove from the end of the chain that does not have the joining pin standing proud.

2 To remove, use a chain tool to push the pin all the way out on Shimano chains, and just short of all the way on other chains, and unthread the chain from the bike. To replace, using the same chain tool, push the dedicated replacement pin (Shimano) into the hole that will join the chain, or, on a new chain, the extended pin that is already half-fitted. Push it

1 Cut the links from the end that does not have the pin standing proud.

2 Use a chain tool to push the pin out and unthread the chain.

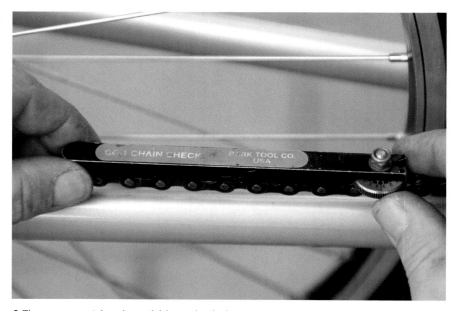

3 There are special tools available to check chain wear.

through until you feel a slight click, and the pin is sticking out evenly on both sides. Take the chain in both hands, one on either side of the new join, and gently flex laterally to remove any chance of a stiff link forming. If you are fitting a Shimano chain, you will now have a piece of pin sticking out on the opposite side of the chain. Break this off with a pair of pliers – it is merely there to guide the pin at the beginning of the process.

3 Check the wear on your chain either with a dedicated tool, or check that it still fits snugly around the big chainring.

Removing a cassette

You should not need to remove the cassette too often but it does make it easier to clean, so knowing how is useful. You will also have to remove it if you need to get at a broken spoke on the drive-side, or service the hub.

1 Remove the quick-release, insert the cassette tool, and loosely replace the quick-release so that it holds the tool in place.

2 Grip one of the larger sprockets with a chain whip, working clockwise, and unscrew the cassette anticlockwise with the cassette tool. The easiest way to do this is with the wheel in front of your knees, with you pushing down on both tools.

3 Slot the cassette back and tighten the lockring by hand. Then tighten using the cassette tool, making sure it is on securely.

1 A dedicated cassette tool is a good investment for a home mechanic.

2 Grip the wheel between your knees and unscrew the cassette.

3 Once the cassette is back in place, tighten the lockring.

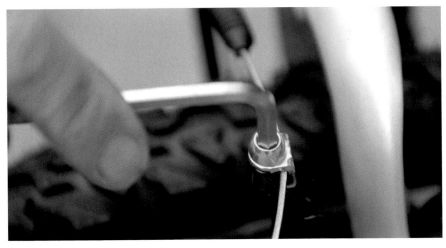

1 Note the routing around the attachment bolt before detaching the cable.

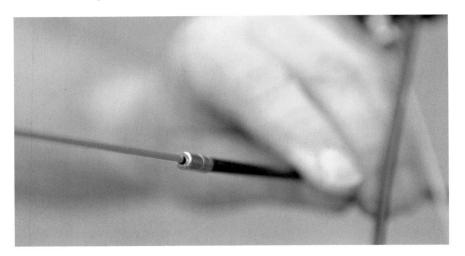

2 Put a drop of oil down the outer cable before you feed the new cable through.

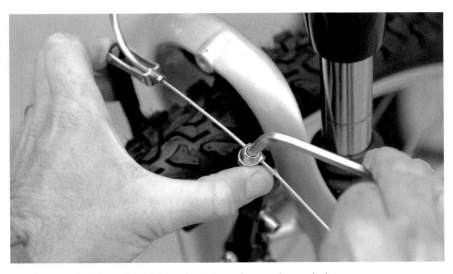

3 Pull in any slack from the cable and retighten the attachment bolt.

Cleaning cables

Cable-operated gear changers have been the standard on mountain bikes since Fisher and Kelly first started converting clunker bikes in the 70s. Modern shifter units are a far cry from the basic thumb-shifters that early bikes came equipped with. They are indexed so that a simple push or pull of a lever engages the next gear precisely and effortlessly. For these systems to work at their optimum, it is important to keep all cables clean, lubricated and running freely.

1 To change the cable in a shifter, click the shifter down into the lowest-tension position, normally the smallest chainring or sprocket (rapid-rise derailleurs will need to be on the biggest sprocket), detach the cable from the derailleur, noting the routing around the attachment bolt, then remove the dust cover from the shifter and take out the remnants of the old cable.

2 Feed the new cable through either brand new, or cleaned and oiled, outers and reattach to the rear derailleur, replacing the cable using the original routing around the clamp bolt.

3 With the bike on the stand, pull the gear cable away from the downtube, as hard as you can, to seat the outer cables. Then loosen the attachment bolt, pull in any slack and retighten. Cut off excess cable and crimp an end-cap on to stop fraying.

1 Adjust the derailleur by using the screw marked L.

2 Insert the cable and tighten, ensuring it follows the same route as the original.

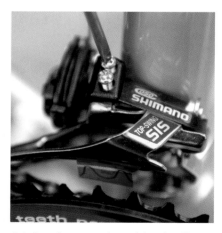

3 Adjust the outer plate of the derailleur using the H screw.

Setting the front derailleur

1 Start with the bike in the smallest chainring and the largest rear sprocket. Using the screw marked L (for low), adjust the derailleur until the inside plate of the derailleur is about 2 mm from the chain.

2 Insert and tighten the cable, rerouting the cable in the same position as the original cable that you removed. Cut off any excess and crimp an end to stop fraying.

3 Shift the chain onto the smallest sprocket and the largest chainring, and use the H (high) screw to adjust the outer plate of the derailleur to about 2 mm clearance between the chain and the outer plate.

Setting the rear derailleur

4 Loosen the cable, use the H screw to adjust the derailleur until the top jockey wheel sits directly below the smallest sprocket, then tighten the cable again.

5 By hand, shift the derailleur across until it is directly below the biggest sprocket, and adjust the L screw accordingly.

6 Check the shifting, and adjust the indexing by turning the adjustment barrel on the back of the derailleur. Turning it clockwise, as you stand behind it, will reduce the tension and adjust the indexing towards the small sprocket; anti-clockwise will increase the tension and cause each shift to throw the chain slightly further towards the large sprocket.

4 Move the rear derailleur so the top jockey wheel sits below the smallest sprocket.

5 Shift the derailleur by hand so that it sits below the biggest sprocket.

6 Turn the adjustment barrel to reduce or increase the tension.

Servicing the brakes

Mountain bike brakes come in two basic forms: disk and V-brake. Disks can either be hydraulically powered – a piston in the lever pushes hydraulic fluid down a tube, which pushes a piston the other end and clamps the brakes closed – or cable actuated, similar to standard brakes. Hydraulic brakes are more powerful and more complicated to service, and are covered next, so let's look at cable disk servicing.

REPLACING BRAKE PADS (EITHER CABLE OR HYDRAULIC) AND ADJUSTING CABLE DISK BRAKES
Remove the split pin that holds the brake pads in and slide the worn pads out. Some brakes have an Allen key that holds the pads in too – remove this as well.

1 With clean hands – any oil at all on the new pads will reduce their effectiveness – slide the new pads in and secure with the same split pins and/or Allen keys. Only buy pads specific to your braking system as they all differ slightly.

2 With the wheel back in the bike, clamp the brake lever tight, undo the bolts holding the calliper to the frame or fork, and retighten. Repeat until the calliper is aligned and the pads don't rub on the rotor when you spin the wheel.

3 If the brakes are only biting with the lever close to the handlebars, adjust the tension in the cable by screwing the adjuster barrel on either the calliper or the lever until the desired position is found.

V-brakes have all but replaced cantilever brakes on non-disk bikes, as they offer better stopping power and better clearance for calf muscles and shins. They are also a lot easier to set up and maintain.

1 Make sure your hands are completely free of oil before sliding the new pads in.
2 Retighten the calliper until it is aligned and the pads don't rub on the rotor.
3 Adjust the tension to your liking by using the adjuster barrel.

1 The internal springs should preferably be in the middle hole on both sides of the frame or fork bosses.

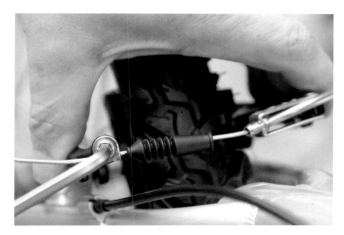

2 When you squeeze the brakes together, they should be vertical where they touch the rim.

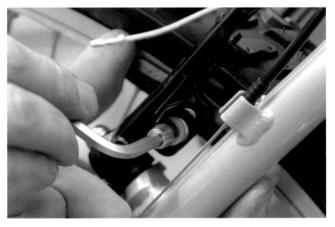

3 Fasten the cable with an Allen bolt. Always leave around 2 mm clearance on either side.

4 Adjust the spring tension on either side by turning the adjuster screws clockwise or anticlockwise.

SETTING UP A V-BRAKE

1 Start by making sure that both sides of the V-brakes are equally tensioned. The exposed end of the internal springs should be in corresponding holes on both sides of the frame or fork bosses – preferably both in the middle hole of the three.

2 Squeeze the brakes together by hand – they should be vertical at the point of contact with the rim. If they are not, adjust the spacing on the brake blocks until they are.

3 Thread the cable through the curved steel guide and the rubber dust boot, and then fasten with the Allen bolt. There should be about 2 mm clearance on each side of the rim. To align the pads properly, slide a piece of thin cardboard in between the back of each block and the rim and pull the brake lever tight. Loosen the Allen bolt that holds the pad on, and once you have aligned the blocks perfectly, tighten again. The cardboard will set the pad so it strikes the rim first, and stop screeching brakes.

4 If one pad touches the rim before the other, adjust the spring tension on one or other side using the adjuster screws. Screw clockwise to move the block away from the rim, and anticlockwise to move it closer to the rim.

BLEEDING THE BRAKES

Hydraulic disk brakes are more powerful and require less maintenance than standard cable systems. The only regular maintenance they require, generally, is keeping disk rotors and brake pads clean, and occasionally replacing the pads.

If you are lucky, you will never have to bleed your hydraulic system, and it is something that should only be done if absolutely necessary. Only consider this maintenance if your brakes are getting progressively more spongy, or need to be pumped before they work. This indicates that there may be air in the system, and to get it out you will need to strip the system down, look for leaks and replace the brake fluid.

Brake fluid – especially non-mineral fluid – is extremely corrosive. Protect everything you don't want damaged with newspaper, and avoid getting it on your hands.

We have chosen to show you how to bleed Shimano Deore XT disk brakes here; if your bike comes with another systems the principle is the same, but the details may differ. Check the owner's manual that came with your brakes or bike for more precise directions.

1 Remove the wheels, put spacers in the callipers so that the brake pistons can't move, remove the grips and turn the lever on the bar so that the reservoir is horizontal.

2 Remove the reservoir cover.

1 After removing the grips, turn the reservoir horizontal and remove the cover.

3 Fit a spanner over the bleed nipple ready to loosen it.

3 Attach a 7 mm spanner to the bleed nipple, then slip one end of the bleed hose over the nipple (**4**). Tie a plastic bag around the other end of the tube. Loosen the bleed nipple one eighth of a turn to open it and allow oil to drain.

5 Keep topping up the oil as it drains, and operate the brake lever a few times (this is where it is important to have the spacer in the calliper so that the blocks do not move). Bubbles will appear in the reservoir. Keep operating the lever until it starts to feel stiff, and bubbles stop forming, topping the oil up as necessary.

2 Once the cover is removed, you will see the brake fluid inside.

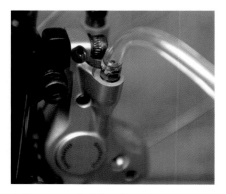

4 Slip one end of the plastic hose over the nipple and fix a bag or bottle on the other.

5 Keep the oil topped up as it drains, and make sure you get air out of the system.

6 Once you have got all the air out of the system, tie the lever to the bar and open and close the bleed nipple a few times at half-second intervals to release any remaining

6 Tie the brake lever to the bar with a rubber band to help expel any air.

1 Old handlebar grips can be removed with a sharp knife and some soapy water.

7 Clean the area around the reservoir very carefully, as some brake fluid is corrosive.

2 To fit the new grip, spray the handlebar with hairspray for lubrication and slide on.

bubbles in the system. Tighten the bleed nipple fully.

7 Replace the reservoir top and screw down carefully. Without letting any air bubbles into the system, remove the tube from the bleed nipple and thoroughly wipe both the lever and calliper areas. Shimano systems should only be filled with mineral oil, but other manufacturers may use DOT brake fluid, which is highly corrosive and will strip paint from frames and completely ruin brake pads if it touches them. So the cleaner you leave the reservoir and handlebar area, the better.

Removing and replacing grips

1 To remove a handlebar grip, work some soapy water under the grip, using a spoke or a thin screwdriver to pry it away from the bar. Twist the grip clockwise and anticlockwise and, as the water gets in under it, it should slide off the bar.

2 Spray the handlebar with hairspray and quickly slide the grip on. The hairspray stays slippery for a short while, but evaporates quickly, leaving the bar, under the grip, dry and sticky. Never use soapy water or a lubricant to apply a grip, as it will take too long to dry and riding a bike with moving grips is dangerous.

For total security with your grips, purchase a set of lockable grips. These have a collar at one or both ends that clamps to the bar via a small Allen bolt, and are not only easy to fit and remove, but also guaranteed to be secure.

Wheel straightening

Wheel straightening is a skill that can be learned at home, with a bit of practice, and can save you both time and money. Spoked wheels are marvels of engineering, but at the same time are fragile, and the amount of abuse mountain bike wheels take means that they need regular maintenance.

A bike wheel is made up of a rim that is suspended around a central hub by tensioned spokes. The spokes coming from the right side of the hub pull the rim to the right, and the spokes from the left side of the hub pull it to the left. Because of the width of the cassette mechanism, there is some offset in the hub, so the right-side spokes are a bit shorter than the left-side ones, and carry more tension. Generally your wheels should come properly built and stay true for many miles, but rough riding can force a wheel to go wobbly, either through rim damage or spokes rattling loose.

1 If you do not have a wheel-truing stand, put your bike in a repair stand or turn it upside down and use the brake blocks as guides.

2 Spin the wheel slowly and see where the rim moves closer to one block or the other.

3 Once you have isolated the section of rim that needs straightening, use a dedicated spoke spanner – your local bike shop will sell you one for your spoke gauge – and tighten one of the spokes coming from the

1 Put your bike in a repair stand and look closely at the brake blocks.

2 Spin the wheel (seen here without the tyre) and note if the rim moves closer to one block.

opposite side of the hub.

Turn the nipple clockwise to tighten, a quarter of a turn at a time, and turn the adjoining spoke, from the other side of the hub, the same amount to keep the wheel circular. Repeat these paired

quarter-turn steps until the rim moves across and the wheel is straighter.

4 Once the rim is no longer touching the brake blocks, tighten the brake cable tension by unscrewing the barrel adjuster, so

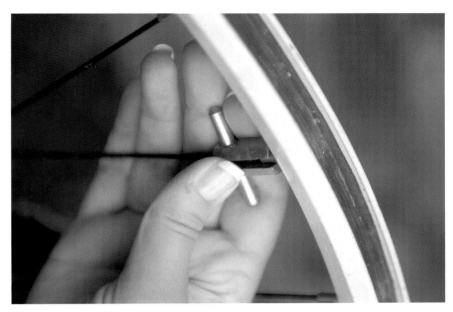

3 Use a spoke spanner to tighten the spokes from the opposite side of the hub.

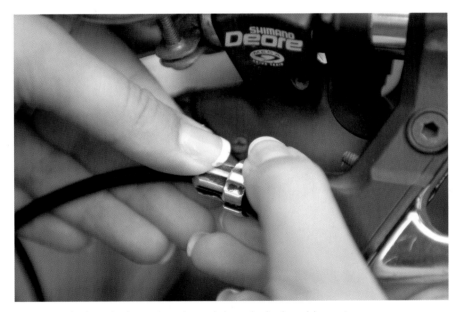

4 Unscrew the barrel adjuster in order to tighten the brake cable tension.

your local mechanic. The principle is the same – tighten spokes to remove hops, loosen them to remove flat spots – but actual deformations in the rim cannot be fixed with spoke tension alone. The rim may need replacing, as a flat spot can cause the brake blocks to foul the tyre wall, causing a blow-out.

Dishing is the technical term for centralizing the wheel in the frame, and if your wheel is off centre, the fix is relatively simple. Loosen all the spokes on the side that is dominant by a quarter turn, and tighten all the spokes a quarter turn on the side towards which you need the rim to move. Repeat until it is centred, then re-true the wheel.

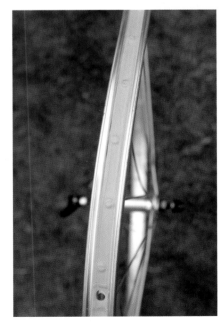

5 A rim that is out of round is a problem perhaps best left to your local bike mechanic to fix.

that the blocks move closer to the rim. Check for spots on the rim that rub, and repeat the truing process. Keep doing this until you can set the blocks to a millimetre or so from the rim without rubbing, then screw the adjuster barrel on the brake cable back in so the blocks are 2–3 mm from the rim.

5 Rims can also go out of round, either through a big hit or spoke tension issues. Without a proper truing-stand, this is a difficult problem to fix, and is best left to

Vital equipment

This is a basic list of items you should carry with you on a normal mountain bike ride. If you are racing in an environment where there are water stops and service points, you might get away with a little less baggage, but remember that mechanicals can and will happen at the most inopportune moment.

3 Two spare tubes Carrying one spare tube almost guarantees you two punctures, but carrying two will make a puncture-free ride a relative certainty.

4 Puncture kit Carry a small puncture kit as a back-up for when you run out of tubes.

6 Hydration pack No matter how short your ride, always take at least a small hydration pack in order to avoid dehydration.

7 Chain tool Never leave on a mountain bike ride without one – the leverage in small gears can snap chains easily.

1 Bike pump With double-headed valve connection so that you can inflate both Schraeder and Presta valves.

2 Tyre levers Tyres can be unbelievably stubborn, especially if your hands are cold, wet or sweaty. Only use plastic tyre levers, as levers made of metal will damage aluminium rims.

5 Multi-tool The most common tools needed out on the trail are 2.5, 4, 5 and 6 mm Allen keys, a flat-head screwdriver and a star (cross-head) screwdriver. Look for a lightweight tool, but one that still is long enough to give you leverage when you need it.

8 Small bottle of lube Especially if it is wet or muddy.

9 Two energy sachets You never know when the ride is going to be longer than planned.

10 ID Never leave home without some form of ID – a piece of paper in a plastic bag will do fine, but make sure you put a friend's or family member's contact details on it. This can double up as a gaiter if you cut the sidewall of a tyre.

11 Lightweight jacket The weather in mountain areas can be unpredictable, and even the warmest of days can turn cold, so always pack a lightweight jacket.

Longer rides and rides into extreme or remote areas require some extra pieces of equipment that will help keep your ride safe and enjoyable:

12 Space blanket This takes up so little room but can be a lifesaver in the event of post-crash shock, or an unexpected night on a mountain.

13 Mini first-aid kit A basic first-aid

kit is vital – make sure there is at least one in your group.

14 Sunblock Needs to be reapplied regularly in the heat as most of it gets sweated off your body.

15 Lip salve Apply regularly on hot days as your breathing robs your lips of moisture, and they spend most of the time in the sun.

16 Energy bars Just in case the ride gets out of hand and takes longer than expected – don't get caught without energy.

17 Spoke spanner At least one spoke spanner per group will be adequate in the event of buckled wheels.

Emergency solutions

By its very nature mountain biking is extremely hard on equipment, and some rides do end in mechanical disaster. Here are some work-arounds for problems you may encounter out on the trail. We can't cover all potential calamities, but these solutions and examples of lateral thinking may help you to prepare for some of problems you may face.

Out of tubes and patches

Stuff the tyre as tightly as you can with leaves and grass. It may not be an ideal way to get home, but it will keep the rim from getting damaged, and, if you ride carefully, it will be a lot quicker than walking.

Above: Stuffing the tyre with leaves and grass in the event of a puncture may earn you some odd looks, but it will get you home faster than walking.

Above: If the rear derailleur should break off, the chain can be shortened to work.

Broken derailleur

When the derailleur goes into the spokes or is broken off by a stick, shorten the chain so that it just fits around the middle chainring and roughly the middle of the cassette. This gear ratio will probably be too big on steep climbs, and too small downhill, but will get you back to where you started.

Forgotten your chain tool and snapped the chain

Shorten it to run as a singlespeed by twisting excess links off and use a piece of fence wire or a spoke to join it. You won't be able to pedal hard on the way back to the car, but you will be able to pedal.

Above: If the chain has snapped, twist any excess links off and use a small piece of wire to join it again. It will not be a strong join, but will suffice in an emergency.

Above: The wheel can be bent back into shape against any solid object.

Broken saddle

Cindy Whitehead once rode 48 miles of a 49 mile race with a broken-off saddle and still won. If you break the top off the rails of a saddle and you're not that tough, wrap the rails with a spare tube. Not great, but better than nothing.

Bent wheel

If you have turned your wheel into a banana shape, straighten it enough to get home by bending it against a tree or rock. If you are riding disks, you will still be able to brake, but V- or cantilever brakes will probably need to be undone to allow the

damaged wheel to turn. Take extra care to ride slowly enough that your bike is still under control.

Above: Bottle-mount bolts can be used to anchor a broken gear cable.

Broken a gear cable

You can either use the adjuster screws to set the derailleur into a position that suits, or use a bottle-mount bolt to anchor the end of the cable once you have tensioned the derailleur into the position you want.

Above: It might not be the height of comfort, but a spare tube can be a makeshift saddle.

Suspension

Suspension revolutionized the mountain bike in the early 90s, and today's forks are arguably more high-tech than the suspension units found on your car. On a car, all they need to do is provide a safe and comfortable ride, but on a bike they need to be light as well, as you are the engine that has to power them.

Fine-tuning your fork can generally be done through the use of rebound and compression dials, and adjusters on the legs of the fork. If you have an air/oil fork, you can adjust the air pressure to increase or decrease the compression of the fork, and change the viscosity of the oil to alter the speed at which it rebounds after compression. Check the manual that came with your fork for pressure settings, and make sure you get a shock pump when you purchase your fork – it will work for your rear suspension unit too if you have a full-suspension bike.

If you have a spring/oil fork, you can adjust the compression by changing to a lighter spring if it is only reacting to big hits, or a heavier one if it is bottoming out too often. Rebound damping is still controlled by the thickness of the oil in the fork.

Day-to-day maintenance of a suspension fork involves little more than wiping the stanchions – the bits that slide in and out – clean after every ride, and checking

1 Drop the wheel out and knock the fork out of the frame to service it properly.

2 Replace the spring and use grease at both ends so that everything runs smoothly.

for excess oil while you are at it. At the same time, check the pressure in the air cartridge, as excess bottoming out can damage the fork.

CHANGING THE SPRING OR ELASTOMER

1 Unscrew the top cap of one leg of the fork, using a ring-end spanner so you don't scratch the fork crown. On most forks, the spring or elastomer can be removed with your fingers or fine-nosed pliers. On some, you may need to unscrew further wedges and stoppers before you can remove them, or unscrew a compression adjuster from the bottom of the fork.

2 Replace the old spring or elastomer, and repeat the process on the other leg if your fork is not oil dampened. Apply some grease to both ends of the elastomer or

3 When you reassemble the bike, make sure that the brake callipers are reattached correctly.

spring so that the fork runs as smoothly as possible.

3 Tighten the top cap on again, carefully as the aluminium threads in the fork crown strip easily, and adjust the preload adjusters to the new sag-level of the new springs or elastomers.

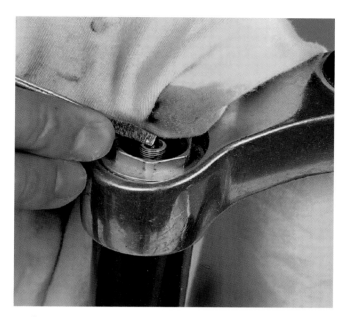

1 *After you have let the air out, remove the top cap from the opposite leg.*

2 *The oil you drain from your fork should be disposed of responsibly, and not poured down a convenient drain.*

3 *Your fork only works correctly with the correct weight of oil; check your manual if unsure.*

CHANGING THE OIL ON AN OPEN BATH AIR FORK

1 Let the air out of the air cartridge and then remove the top cap from the opposite leg, being careful not to scratch the crown.

2 Drain the oil into a container and dispose of it in an environmentally responsible manner.

3 Pour new oil – your manual will tell you what viscosity to use – into the open leg, making sure the fork is completely vertical. Tap the fork gently with a mallet to remove any remaining air bubbles and replace the top cap carefully. Re-inflate the air cartridge to the required level of sag.

Rear suspension units are generally self-contained and are not serviceable, except by the agents. You can keep them running better, for longer, by making sure you wipe the piston clean after every ride. While you are at it, check for abnormal amounts of oil seeping out of the shock. There should be a little bit for lubrication, but if the amount increases significantly, have it checked. Always make sure you have enough air pressure – regular bottoming out can damage the internals of a suspension unit beyond repair.

The pivot points and mounting points will either move on bearings or bushings. Lubricate bearings after every ride to stop creaking and increase efficiency. Never apply grease or lubricant to nylon bushings, however, as they are designed to run dry, and will wear badly if lubricated.

RIDING POSITION

Setting up your mountain bike properly before you start riding it is vital if you want to get maximum power and enjoyment. There is a basic system for finding the correct balance between power, aerodynamics and comfort, with minor tweaks for the various disciplines of the sport. Remember that it is just that: basic. You will need to tweak and fiddle with minor settings on the bike for your body. You may have longer thighs – so slide the seat back a bit – or a short torso – look for a shorter stem – but as a starting point, follow these procedures. There are professional bike set-up centres in most big cities, and if you are serious about racing it is probably best to have one of these fine-tune your position on the bike. Even if it is a costly exercise, it may transform your racing to correct errors caused by ignoring your body's particular shape when setting up your bike.

The first step is making sure you buy the correct size of bike. For a road bike, you would measure your inseam, from your crotch to the floor, and multiply this value, in centimetres, by 0.66. The easiest way to measure this is to stand barefoot with your back to a wall, feet slightly apart. Slide a hardcover book, spine flat against the wall, up between your legs until it feels like you are sitting on a saddle. Have somebody mark the wall with a pencil at the highest point of the book. Measure from the mark to the ground. This

formula gives you an accurate idea of your road bike size, and mountain bikes run 8–10 cm (3–4 in) smaller than road bikes. Sizing a mountain bike is not an exact science, as different manufacturers spec different top tube lengths for similar sized bikes, so once you have a rough idea, shop around and try bikes until you find one that works for you.

The next measurement to obtain is the saddle height, using the same value you found measuring your inner leg, multiplied by 0.883, measured from the centre of the bottom bracket axle to the top of the saddle, along the line of the seat tube. This will give you an approximate saddle height, but it is important to fine-tune it. Wearing your cycling shoes and shorts, and clipped into your pedals, position the cranks at six o'clock and twelve o'clock. The straighter leg should have a bend of between 25 and 30 degrees at the knee. Mountain bikers will generally move towards a thirty degree bend, as a lower seat offers better stability, but try not to move out of the 25–30 zone as lower seat heights can cause knee problems.

The third step is to set the fore-aft adjustment of the saddle. Wearing cycling shorts, and clipped into your pedals, move one foot to the three o'clock position. Have a helper run a plumbline from the front of your kneecap, hanging down to bisect

Above: With feet at six o'clock and twelve o'clock, your legs should have a bend of 25–30 degrees.

the pedal axle. Stronger, more experienced riders can slide the seat back a bit more, but no more than half a centimetre behind the axle, for more power. The saddle should be level – use a spirit level if you are not sure – or tilted slightly upwards. Nose-down will see you sliding towards the bars, and your shoulders and arms will tire quickly from holding you up on longer rides.

The final step to your ideal bike position is getting your upper body into a position that will be a compromise between power, freedom to breathe and comfort. This is not an exact science and is down to personal preference, but look for a position that will allow you to sit comfortably on long rides, with your arms and shoulders relaxed and elbows slightly bent. Handlebars should be between 2.5–5 cm (1–2 in) below the saddle.

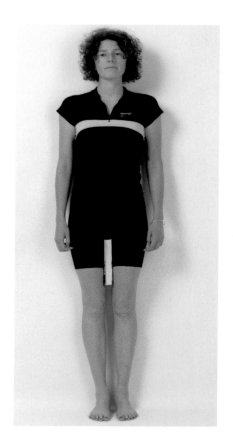

Above: To find out what size bike you should be riding, use a hardback book and mark the wall where it reaches.

Above: This helmet is not being worn correctly. It is too far back on her head and will not protect her in a crash.

Above: Correctly fitted, a helmet should be horizontal with the straps fitting snugly under the chin.

Helmet fit

Fitting your helmet correctly is vital to your safety. It may take a few minutes of fiddling with straps to get it right, but you should only have to do it once to set it up correctly.

Start by buying the right size helmet – it should fit your head snugly and not shift around at all. With the rear adjuster mechanism tightened up, it should almost stay on your head if you lean forward. Adjust the straps so that they fit snugly to your face and are not loose. The helmet should be horizontal, as having it too far back on your head will expose your temples in the event of a crash.

With the straps snug, adjust the chin strap as tight as is comfortable – you should be able to get a couple of fingers between it and your chin, no more – as this will

Above: The cleat on the bottom of your shoe should be positioned correctly in order to avoid injury.

Above: The ball of your foot should be directly over the axle if you are to get the most power out of your stroke.

person. A good place to start is to look at the angle of your feet when you walk, or how they hang when dangling off a low wall, in order for you to get an idea of which way they are pointing. Position the cleat so that your feet are at a similar angle to this – for most people it is with your heels slightly inwards – and with your shoe as close to the crank as you can without your ankle touching.

Brake levers

Set your brake levers so that when you are sitting in your normal position, with your hands on the levers and fingers extended, a straight line runs through your arm, wrist and fingers. Lower than this, and you will struggle to get full power, setting them higher will put undue pressure on your wrists.

ensure the helmet stays in the correct position, no matter how hard you hit it in a crash.

Pedal position

Positioning your foot on the pedal, or more accurately positioning the cleat on the bottom of the shoe, is critical to getting maximum power from your pedal stroke, and to avoiding injury. There are two areas to look after – fore-aft adjustment, and the angle of your foot.

Fore-aft adjustment is simple: the ball of your foot should be directly over the pedal axle. Alignment of your feet will differ from person to

Above: Setting your brakes too high will put pressure on your wrists and be uncomfortable after a day in the saddle.

Above: If you brake levers are set too low, you will not be able to use them with full power.

Setting up the suspension

Setting up your suspension properly is relatively simple to do, but you will need to enlist the help of somebody to measure sag levels. Both your air forks and your rear suspension units will have recommended sag levels in the manuals that will have been supplied with your bike and, while it is generally acceptable to inflate the cartridge to the pressure recommended for your weight, it is only a rule of thumb. Customizing your suspension setup will transform your ride.

Suspension forks have two controllable actions as they react to changes in surface beneath your wheels: the first is the compression, which is how much the fork stanchions slide into the legs of the fork when you hit a bump; and the second is the rebound, which is the rate at which the stanchions return to their original position after compression.

Compression is adjusted, in coil-spring or elastomer forks, by changing either the spring or the elastomer for a different grade. If your fork bottoms out regularly, you need a heavier spring or elastomer. If it never bottoms out, chances are the spring is too stiff and you need a lighter one. Air forks adjust the compression through increased or decreased pressure in the air chamber.

Rebound dampening is controlled by the weight of oil used

1 To set the fork sag, fasten a cable tie around one of the stanchions. Make sure it is tied tightly enough so that it doesn't slide down of its own accord.

2 Sit on the bike carefully and put both feet on the pedals. The fork will compress and the cable tie will move – measure the distance and adjust the sag accordingly.

Above: A shock pump is a vital piece of equipment if you want to adjust the sag on your rear suspension.

in the dampening system, which can be changed using the methods outlined on pages 92–93, and then fine-tuned using the adjusters found at the top (or bottom) of one of the fork legs. The best way to set the rebound properly is to find a long washboard section (level ground with a rough, bumpy surface) and ride it a few times, adjusting the damping each time. If the fork gradually nose-dives, or the rear shock gets progressively shorter in its travel, the rebound is too slow and is not returning to its original position fast enough. If the front of the bike judders and is bouncing around excessively, slow the dampening down a bit. Keep adjusting until you find a balance between the two.

Sag is the amount your fork or rear shock moves when you simply sit on the bike. All suspension units are designed to have sag – forks generally sag 25 per cent of the total travel of the fork, and to specific manufacturer's specifications on rear units.

SETTING FORK SAG

1 Put a cable tie tightly around one of the stanchions – you will use this to measure the travel of the fork, so make it tight enough that it does not slide down of its own accord.

2 Climb onto the bike – putting it on an indoor trainer with a wedge under the front wheel (to keep the bike level) will make this process easier – in your normal cycling kit and with both feet on the pedals.

Try to climb on carefully, moving the fork as little as possible. The fork will compress under your weight, and the cable tie will be moved. Climb off just as carefully and measure the distance the cable tie has moved.

Increase or decrease the pressure, depending on whether there was too much or too little sag, aiming for 25 per cent of the total travel.

SETTING SAG ON THE REAR SUSPENSION

3 Measure the distance between your shock's two mounting bolts,

centre to centre, without you sitting on the bike.

Climb onto the bike as gently as you can and have a helper measure the distance between the centres of the mounting bolts with you in your normal position on the bike.

4 The second measurement should be somewhere between a quarter and a third of the first, but each shock has its own ideal range, so check the manual for details. Adjust the pressure in the shock by adding or removing air in an air shock, or changing the weight of the spring in a coil-over shock.

3 To set the sag on the rear suspension, measure the distance between the two mounting bolts of the shock. Do this first off the bike and then again when you are sat on it.

4 Adjust the pressure as necessary using your shock pump, adding or removing air as needed.

Correct bike set-ups

CROSS-COUNTRY BIKES

Cross-country racing is the purest form of the sport and as such is all about efficiency and speed, with comfort taking a back seat. The frame angles on the bikes are steep, almost as steep as road bikes, and short stems, low-travel forks, no rear suspension and low bars make for fast, brutal machines.

Because cross-country races rarely last longer than a couple of hours, the emphasis of the set-up is on power at all costs. Saddle height will be as high as a road bike, with most riders sacrificing a tiny bit of control on the steeper descents for extra power from the legs. To this end, many riders slide the saddle back on its rails, so that the kneecap is a centimetre or so behind the pedal axle. This allows their strengthened quadriceps muscles – the most powerful in the legs – to gain some extra leverage, but at the risk of knee injuries.

The same is true for the fore-aft position of the cleat, with a popular choice being to move the cleat forward so that the ball of the foot is a small distance behind the pedal axle. This gives extra leverage with the calf muscles, which is fine over short distances and if you are a highly trained athlete, but if you are none of the above, don't risk injury; rather leave the ball of your foot directly over the axle.

The cockpit area on a cross-country bike is shorter than on a normal mountain bike, and the handlebars are considerably lower, as riders look for aerodynamic advantage on the fast courses this type of racing produces. Bar ends can be positioned close to horizontal, as you will be using them for leverage when you stand on the steep, short climbs.

DOWNHILL BIKES

The major objective with positioning on a downhill bike is for maximum control, so bars are higher than on a cross-country machine, and much wider allowing for better leverage to man-handle the bike through technical sections. The position on a downhill is vastly different from any other bike. The saddle is way too low to pedal properly, and any pedalling is done standing up. Cleat position, if the rider chooses to use clipless pedals instead of platform pedals, will be

Above: *Cross-country riding focuses on speed and efficiency, meaning that the set-up will not be the most comfortable.*

Above: Women have shorter torsos, shorter lower legs and longer femurs than men, meaning that their bikes should be set up very differently.

Left: Downhill riding is all about speed and control. The saddle is not designed for comfort as it is very rarely used, – any pedalling is done standing up.

as neutral as possible, with the ball of the foot directly over the pedal axle.

SINGLESPEED BIKES

Singlespeed bikes are difficult to ride, as you are virtually guaranteed to be either in too big or too small a gear. To get up steep trails, singlespeed riders spec short stems and wide riser bars so that they can use the extra leverage to force the bike up the hills. Saddle height is ideally similar to that on a

cross-country bike, although if you are riding mainly steep, rocky, rooty trails you may want to drop it slightly. Keep the fore-aft positions of both the saddle and the cleats neutral

WOMEN RIDERS

The riding position for women differs from that for men, in all categories, in two distinct ways. First, women have a shorter torso and weaker upper body, so the bike should have a shorter top tube, a

shorter stem and a slightly higher bar/stem combo. A slightly more upright position will also shift the weight from the soft tissue areas to the pelvic bones, a better option for all but the shortest rides.

The second major difference is that women tend to have longer femurs and shorter lower legs, and to maximize the advantage of this difference, many female riders slide their saddles back a centimetre or so. This lets the longer, stronger quad muscles work best.

Above: *Bikes for endurance races should be set up to give more control and comfort on all-day races.*

ENDURANCE BIKES

The set-up on mountain bikes that are going to be ridden in all-day epics, marathon races or stage races needs to be as neutral as possible. Experimenting with position is fine if you are racing for only two hours, but over the course of a day of hard riding, minor discomfort can turn to injury very quickly.

Saddle height for endurance, marathon and all-mountain riders is quite similar, and is slightly lower than the equivalent cross-country position. This allows riders more movement in and around the saddle, making it possible to have

more control on the downhills, especially when tired at the end of a long ride. The disadvantage of this lower position is that it increases the strain on the knee joints, so make sure you don't drop the seat too much.

Cleat position should be dead centre above the pedal axle, as you will already be putting strain on your knees with the lower seating position. Fore-aft position of the saddle should be neutral, with your kneecap directly above the pedal axle.

Endurance riders look for a slightly longer position on the bike than cross-country riders, and

normally with slightly higher handlebars so that the lower back is less strained on all-day rides. Along with this slightly raised stem come longer bar ends than found on a cross-country machine, offering more hand positions for greater comfort. Angle them slightly higher than on a cross-country machine, as you will be using them more sitting down than standing up and if they are set too low, you will put strain on your wrists.

TANDEM BIKES

Sizing and position on a tandem is challenging, as the range of sizes available is not as comprehensive as that of single bikes. Start by making sure that the front rider – the captain – is sized as close to his normal mountain bike as possible. Sizing on the rear – for the stoker – is less critical, as adjustable handlebar stems and seatposts will allow you to fit anybody within a few inches of the theoretically correct size.

Once you have found the right size bike for the captain, the position is very similar to what you would find on a marathon or endurance single bike. The only major difference will be a slightly longer stem to give the captain a bit more leverage to muscle the tandem through the corners. Keep the fore-aft position as neutral as possible, with your kneecap over the pedal axle, and the same holds true for the cleat position.

Saddle height can be marginally lower than on a cross-country bike, mainly because you will need to be able to move around on the tandem to help it around corners and over obstacles. Try to keep it as close as you can to optimal height, though, as tandem riding is tough on the body and you want to avoid extra strain.

Bar ends on the front bars should be raised slightly as you are going to be using them almost exclusively sitting down.

To position the stoker, start by getting the saddle height right – cross-country height is fine, the stoker is primarily there to produce power – and a neutral fore-aft position for both saddle and cleats. Now slide the adjustable stem in and out until the stoker feels comfortable with the length. The stoker can sit slightly higher and shorter than on a single bike as they will not need to steer, and are in the slipstream of the captain at all times.

Below: The bar ends on a tandem bike should be slightly raised – they will rarely be used standing up.

RIDING TECHNIQUES

For most riders new to the sport, the biggest hurdle is getting past the apparent danger of it. Speak to a non-mountain biker and chances are you will be told that you are entering the realm of the reckless and foolhardy. Even road cyclists who have never ventured off-road long enough to find out for themselves will tell you how dangerous it is, yet they are prepared to share the road with cars, trucks and pedestrians. Mountain biking has one huge advantage over road cycling in this regard: generally, you are the master or mistress of your own fate.

Above: The key to mastering new skills is to experiment on different terrains, ride with more experienced cyclists and observe.

First steps in mastering the trail

Crashing a mountain bike is more often than not a result of human error, whether it is a lack of attention to maintenance, not reading the terrain on which you are riding, or trying to ride a trail which you don't yet have the experience to master. You are unlikely to have to deal with cars, or have a driver fail to see you. It's just you, your bike and nature.

There are two basics that will make mountain biking safe and fun, and they are so simple that you cannot fail to remember them: momentum is your friend, and you have more control than you think, so commit and stick with it.

Momentum is a remarkable ally on the mountain bike. Experienced riders use it for the most part subconsciously, and will instinctively roll over roots, logs and other small obstacles that will scare the living daylights out of you the first time you venture out. Half the reason you will struggle with these small obstacles is hesitance, and the only way you will overcome this fear is to conquer it in stages. Find a grass field and a series of obstacles. Start with small sticks, gradually increasing the size as you ride at them and over them. Ride slightly faster than walking pace, building up to riding over something the size of a brick. You will be able to ride over this size of object without danger of crashing.

Once you have mastered keeping your momentum going over these smaller obstacles, you can practise lifting the front wheel to help you over slightly larger objects. Start with the same brick. Your goal is to get the front wheel off the ground and over the brick without touching it. Don't worry about the back wheel – it will follow you. At a walking pace, ride towards the brick. As the front wheel is about to hit the brick, give a sharp pedal stroke and gently pull up on the bars. The front wheel should pop up and over the brick. Experiment with different gears until you can intuitively select the right gear at a variety of speeds.

Once you are confident of doing this, start practising on larger objects. Skilled riders can tackle obstacles up to a foot high. However, be aware that the chain ring could foul on larger objects.

Overcoming obstacles

You don't need to be a lunatic observed-trials rider to ride over a fallen tree or up an earthen bank. A combination of technique and commitment will amaze your riding partners and keep you on the bike when you would normally be hike-a-biking. The following technique is best performed on a log, where catching the chain ring will do minimal damage, but is also good for rock ledges and high kerbs. Just make sure you can clear the chain ring on hard surfaces.

1 Getting over larger obstacles is a little more complicated and relies on a combination of momentum and skill. The first step is to roll towards the log at a gentle pace, marginally faster than walking pace. As you get to the log, lift the front wheel onto the log and stand up on the pedals, moving your weight forwards.

2 Keep pedalling, push forwards on the handlebars and allow your momentum and pedalling action to roll the bike over the log.

3 Once the front wheel is back on the ground, move your weight all the way back so you don't pitch over the bars. The back wheel will roll off the log and land safely behind you.

Right: More than a fancy trick, the ability to ride over obstacles this big will help you to clear the gnarliest of trails with relative ease.

Above: *Use the front brake to stop, then turn the front wheel about 45 degrees and rock forwards and back on the pedals.*

Above: *Learn to track stand in both directions for even better trail control.*

TRACK STANDS

The next 'trick' to learn is one that seems a little showy at first, but will stand you in good stead when you are riding tight, technical trails. Track stands originated in track racing, where match-sprinters would spend minutes at a time standing still in an attempt to force their opponent to take the lead in the race to the line. On the road, it is one way to avoid unclipping at stop signs and traffic signals, but it is on the mountain bike that the track stand is particularly useful.

Because the overall speed in mountain biking is so much slower than road biking, you will rely more on balance and low-speed control, so the ability to ride as slowly as possible, and even stop without falling over, is critical to overall control. Whether you need to re-adjust your centre of gravity to climb a hairpin bend or change a line while descending a series of tight switchbacks, being able to stop, reposition and then get started again without falling over can be critical.

Start by finding a gentle uphill slope and roll up it in a light gear until you come to a halt. Turn the front wheel slightly, with cranks level and the wheel turned away from the foremost foot. Dab the front brake so that the bike stops, and allow it to roll backwards a few inches. Slight pressure on the pedals will roll you forwards, and you will eventually find a balance between reversing, braking and pedalling. When you are ready to ride off again, straighten the bars, and ride off in your new chosen direction. With practice, you will be able to balance for a few minutes uphill, and momentarily downhill, helping you gather your thoughts and pick the right line on technical trails.

BUNNY HOPS

The bunny hop is an essential mountain biking skill that will transform your riding. It will allow you to clear smaller obstacles without having to slow down to perform the up-and-over combinations detailed in previous pages. It is also useful for jumping over small holes and rain ruts. There are two key elements to bunny hopping: timing and technique. Getting the timing right is a matter of practising as often as you can. The best way to learn is using a small tree branch or a brick, placed in an open space.

1 Ride at speed and, as you get to the obstacle, crouch slightly over the bars. Straighten up and pull on the bars, all the while moving your weight towards the back wheel. The front wheel will lift off the ground and clear the obstacle; this is where the timing comes in – as you practise more you will learn exactly when to lift the wheel.

2 Now lift the back wheel. You do this by pulling back and up on the pedals – your cranks should be level throughout this movement – bringing the rear of the bike up to the same level as the front.

3 The final stage and, it might argued, the most important of the

Right: Leaning how to bunny hop over small obstacles is a great skill to master, and one that will stand you in good stead on any trail. Timing is crucial, though – practise this technique as much as you can until the timing comes naturally.

Above: Leaning away from the camber feels unnatural but works best.

Above: Ride as upright as you dare and trust the tyres.

bunny hop is the landing. The ideal landing sees both wheels touching the ground at the same time, with the rider's arms and legs compressed slightly to absorb the impact. Many experienced riders land the rear wheel marginally before the front, allowing them to cushion the blow further and focus

on landing the front wheel exactly where they want. Once you have the bike under control, ride away and look for your next obstacle.

OFF-CAMBER CONTROL

Off-camber surfaces are some of the trickiest you will come across. Presuming you can pedal without clipping the slope with the inside pedal, lean away from the slope. Your instinct will be to lean into it, but by doing so you run the risk of clipping the pedal. Leaning out will give you the clearance you need and allow you to keep riding for longer.

If the slope is so severe that you cannot pedal, the choices are either to run with the bike (make sure you are upslope from the bike in case you slip or trip) or stay in the saddle and drag yourself along skateboard-style.

WHEELIES

Wheelies are considerably more useful off-road than they first seem. Those that can't get this 'trick' right will tell you that it is just showing off, but used to their full potential out on the trail they can be extremely useful. Whether it is riding through a large puddle without having to check its depth first, or keeping your front wheel clean through patches of mud, the ability to float through tricky sections is a big advantage.

The principle is quite simple, it just takes a lot of practice. Find a gradual slope and ride up it, in a

Above: Keep on the balance point by feathering the back brake.

light gear, at walking pace. Pedal hard and pull up and back on the bars, so that the front wheel lifts off the ground. Keep pedalling and the wheel will stay in the air. Now the tricky part. If you start to go over backwards too far, gently pull on the back brake and the front wheel will drop sharply. The trick is to keep the bike on what is called the balance point – the point at which you are no longer falling over backwards, but the front wheel is not dropping either – by pedalling or braking accordingly.

Experienced exponents of the skill are able to do this downhill, too, and without pedalling, just by shifting their weight, in what is known as a coaster wheelie. For general mountain biking, which shuns showboating, the ability to hold the front wheel up for six pedal strokes can prove an advantage in the trickier sections of a trail.

Different terrain

Part of the attraction of riding bicycles off-road is the unpredictability offered. This is never more true than in regard to the variety of terrain that may be encountered, often on the same ride. Mud, rocks, sand, snow, roots, tar, gravel, ice – each has its own peculiar way of trying to unseat you, but with the right levels of commitment and momentum, as well as sensible equipment choice, nearly all surfaces are quite rideable.

Mud The key to riding in mud is to keep your actions as smooth as possible. Stay seated, but keep your centre of gravity towards the middle of the bike and pedal

Above: Sandy surfaces can be very tricky to ride over.

Above: Mud is an integral part of the off-road experience.

smoothly in a light gear. When you exit a muddy stretch, remember that the tyres will be clogged for a few yards on the cleaner surface and could be quite slippery. A couple of bunny hops will shake the worst out of the knobbles, but be cautious with any cornering.

Sand This is the bane of most mountain bikers' existences, especially in drier climes. Event organizers dislike it less than the riders, so it is important to know how to ride the stretches you will inevitably encounter. On the flat and uphill, keep your weight neutral over the middle of the bike and pedal in a medium gear. The key is to keep pedalling smoothly to stop the wheel spinning, and

Above: *Cold weather means slower reaction times and slippery surfaces.*

Above: *Bare rock offers great traction, both for tyres and skin!*

keep the bars as straight as you can using your shoulders and upper body to guide rather than turning. Rely on your momentum to carry you where you want to go rather than steering, as the sand will force the front wheel to dart about.

Snow Riding in the snow offers two potential problems: generally, you cannot see the ground surface

below the snow, and snow and water build up on your rims. The former is negated by riding cautiously and presuming the surface is slippery and muddy until proven otherwise, while the latter will require you to gently and regularly apply the brakes to clear accumulated water and stop it turning to ice.

Rocks Loose rocks can be daunting to ride, but as long as they are relatively small – the size of a tennis ball or smaller – you should get through them without incident. Stand out of the saddle, weight neutral, and in a medium gear. Use your shoulders to guide the bike rather than steering through the handlebars, and expect the bike to buck around a bit as rocks slip out from under the wheels. As long as you maintain momentum, this apparent lack of control will not be problematic.

Roots There are two basic rules to help you through sections of the trail covered with roots. First, try to ride over them at ninety degrees to the root – this will stop your front wheel sliding left or right as it hits. Roots are slippery when dry and lethal when wet, so the second rule is to wheelie the front of the bike over them and let the back wheel take care of itself, which it will comfortably. Extended sections of roots will require close investigation and you will either have to plan a safe route, or run the bike through if they are too wet and slippery.

Above: *Smooth, gravelly singletrack is the holy grail of off-road surfaces.*

Gravel Gravel roads form the mainstay of the mountain biking experience, and are also the highest-speed surface you will ride on. You will seldom ride faster than 20 or 25 kph (12`–15 mph) on a singletrack path, but on a wide-open forest road, speeds of 60 kph (37 mph) or more are quite possible. The margin for error at this speed is small, so it is important to consider your speed at all times – make sure you have enough reaction time to jump, brake and steer, no matter what is hidden around the next corner. Always keep your movements and actions smooth and controlled – sudden changes in direction and violent braking are sure to cause crashes.

Going up

More than any other discipline of cycling, mountain biking demands a mastery over gravity. Climbs tend to be longer, steeper and more technically challenging, forcing riders not only to be fit and strong, but mentally agile too. Where their road-bound cousins can focus purely on riding fast, mountain bikers need to manage both themselves and the physical and natural world.

In general, we can break off-road climbing down into three distinct categories: open-road, singletrack and technical. Each has its own separate set of skills and techniques, and each will be thrown into any decent event course in varying quantities. Because you will be spending more time climbing than descending, by nature of the lower speeds involved in fighting gravity, it is worth learning to maximize your ascending prowess.

Much of your climbing will be done on grades that are similar to those you would find on the road bike, where the course is not steep enough to cause traction problems for the rear wheel. Forest roads and mountain passes will test you more physically than technically, so a positive attitude and fitness will carry you to the top of all but the meanest ascents.

Body position is important here – you want to be sitting over the centre of the bike, arms and shoulders relaxed and neck loose. You will be spending a fair amount of time in this position – even a gradual 5 km (3 mile) climb will take 15 to 20 minutes – so avoid a death-grip on the bars, but rather relax on the bike.

Start the climb at a pace you know you can maintain for the full duration. If you don't know the area, keep to a pace you can sustain for half an hour: you can always increase your efforts towards the top, but start off too quickly and you stand a chance of slowing to a walking pace, or even walking,

Left: *Alternate between sitting and standing on long climbs to break the monotony and give your legs a brief rest.*

Above: *When climbing seated, slide back on the saddle to maximize power output from your quadriceps.*

Above: *Cross-country racing calls for plenty of full-tilt, out-of-the-saddle climbing, hence the need for great physical fitness for this discipline.*

before you reach the top. Riding long climbs with other people can be very tricky, as you will each have a different comfort level on any particular gradient. It is important to ride at your own level, or you run the risk of ruining the rest of your ride trying to keep up. Riding in a more comfortable, restrained fashion may yet mean you can close in on your riding buddies over the duration of the climb. Pacing yourself is critical, as is standing on the pedals occasionally to change your position slightly and rest a few key muscles, as well as helping you adjust to slight changes in gradient.

Keeping your cadence fairly high will help in two ways on longer, more open climbs: it will keep your legs rested and ready for action later on in the ride; and it will give

you some extra momentum to roll through changes in ground surface and gradient.

Switchback corners can be tricky on these longer, more open climbs. The temptation is to take the shortest line possible, but a better option is to stick to the outside of the corner all the way through. You

will ride marginally further, but almost all switchbacks are cambered, and the most constant gradient is found on the outer edges. On the very inside of the corner you will need to climb an extra-steep section, which could rob you of momentum and energy.

Above: *Climbing steep slopes on good surfaces is as simple as standing up and hammering it.*

Getting steeper

Steeper climbs demand a different attitude, both mentally and with regard to your position on the bike. You are unlikely to find extended climbs where you are struggling for rear wheel traction; what are more likely to be encountered are short, sharp peaks in the route profile. Learning to get over these without having to get off and push will save you a lot of time.

Body position is critical. You need to be far enough back on the bike to stop the rear wheel spinning out on loose terrain, yet you still need to keep some weight on the front of the bike to stop the front wheel from lifting off the ground. Shifting back in the saddle and concentrating on pulling back on the bars, instead of up, will help, but practice will ultimately give you the best position for tackling the really steep terrain.

Bar ends are a great help here, as they allow you to spread your weight more over both wheels, as well as offering a little more leverage.

Above: *On loose terrain, shift your weight over the rear wheel to prevent slipping.*

Above: Long climbs need patience, planning and a good deal of mental and physical strength.

Left: Climbing always hurts, but bar ends can help by giving you more leverage.

Standing in these conditions can be tricky, as it immediately unweights your rear wheel. Make sure the transition between sitting and standing is as smooth as possible, or the rear wheel will spin out and you will lose all forward momentum. Stay seated as much as you can, but if you must stand – and it often helps to turn over a slightly heavier gear, giving you more control and speed – keep it smooth and controlled.

Gear choice can be critical here too, as opting for a slightly heavier gear may help you with traction control. A very easy gear might seem like a good idea, and will certainly be easier on your legs in the long run, but it also gives you too much leverage over the rear wheel, making it easy to spin out on the loose stuff. A slightly harder gear will keep the rear tyre firmly dug into the terrain. Again, this is where bar ends will come in handy, as they will give you extra leverage and allow you to man-handle the bike in a bigger gear than normal.

Singletrack

Singletrack is the most rewarding, yet most demanding of all the aspects of off-road climbing. Paths and trails tend to be narrow and vary in gradient and under-wheel conditions, sometimes from metre to metre. The keys to riding swiftly up singletrack are to plan your line and effort, and to keep your momentum going. More often than not, once you have stopped riding on a singletrack section, it is virtually impossible to get going again, so keeping the bike rolling forward is vital.

Planning your route is critical. Often, you will not have the luxury of choosing exactly where you will put your wheels, as the trail will be just wide enough for you and the bike, but you will need to be looking ahead at all times, making sure you are aware of what is happening fifteen or twenty feet in front of you. If you discover a 30 cm (12 in) log only once it is under your front wheel, your chances of getting over it in one piece are minimal, and the chances of getting over the next one ten feet later are zero. You should always be focusing on the obstacles ahead, letting your bike handling skills and momentum carry you over the obstacle at hand.

Body position will vary constantly on singletrack, but keeping a neutral position will let you change your attitude, seated or standing, as the conditions demand. Generally, you will find yourself sitting a bit further back than on long, open climbs, and riding in a slightly bigger gear, which will let you make changes in speed more easily.

Cornering in singletrack also requires planning and a very careful choice of line. The corners generally link more level sections of trail and, as such, will combine steeper gradients with changes in

Left and above: Whether you are on a downhill run (top) or a cross-country course (bottom), the same neutral position on the bike should be used. This allows you to sit or stand as needed.

direction and often loose, disturbed trail surfaces. Pick the line you intend to ride – keeping to the outside of the corner is often smoother and easier – and stick to it. A slightly higher gear and a bit of effort will keep your momentum up, and you can always recover a little on the next straight bit of trail.

One vital skill to learn for successful singletrack riding is clearing step-ups and logs. Often, maintenance crews will use logs placed at right angles to the direction of travel to stop riders and rain carrying the trail downhill. The sand and gravel will pack up on the high side of these logs, but not on the low side, creating a drop-off if you are descending and a step-up if you are going the other way. Most riders can ride over step-ups if they are a few inches high. With your weight forward on the bike, wheelie and deposit the front wheel on the log. Stop pedalling and, as the back wheel gets to the log, push forward on the bars and lift the pedals with your feet. The back wheel will pop up and over. By this time, most of your momentum will have been stolen by the log, so you will need to focus on your balance and pedal off in a controlled manner.

Right: *Keep looking as far down the trail as you can.*

Going down

Rapidly descending on wide-open forest roads is one of the most thrilling things you will ever experience on a mountain bike. Unfortunately, it is also one of the areas you need to focus on doing well, as the high speeds involved leave you very little margin for error. Always err on the side of caution, and always keep within the limits of your bike and your abilities.

Body position is fairly simple in these high-speed situations. Keeping your weight a little further back than usual will let you lift the front wheel over rain-bars and small obstacles in the trail, and will let you control your speed using the back brake (but gently, so you don't skid). Cornering at speed will require a slightly different position. You will need to slide forward a bit on the bike to allow the front wheel to dig in a bit more, letting it grip better and letting you use the more powerful front brake a little more. Just remember that this will unweight the back wheel slightly and it will want to slide about, but rather that than have the front wheel do the same.

Taking off

The most critical skill to learn for most riders is high-speed jumping. If you are descending at more than 30 kph (19 mph) – and you will often be hurtling down more open roads at speeds closer to 60 kph (37 mph) – you will simply not have time to stop and gently lift the front wheel over obstacles on the road. Whether you are faced with a tree branch or a rain rut in the road, the ability to lift the bike over small obstacles is a necessity, and the technique for doing so is very simple.

Above: For the best descent, keep your weight as far back as you can and try not to use the front brake too much on the really steep parts.

Left: Jumping is an advanced skill that demands total commitment and bravery. Once you have spotted a suitable take-off and landing point, approach the obstacle and pull back and up on the bars (far left). Lift the back wheel by pulling back and up on the pedals (left), lift both wheels to the same level (below), then try and land both wheels at the same time.

Your first job is to identify a suitable take-off spot and a suitable landing spot. Often, you will not have a problem here, as a branch across the road will not have altered the road surface conditions before or after the obstacle, but if you are wanting to jump over a rain rut or a pot hole, make sure you know exactly what lies beyond it.

As you approach the obstacle, pull back and up on the bars and shift your weight back on the bike. The front wheel will lift up and over the obstacle. Almost simultaneously, pull back and up on the pedals, lifting the back wheel up to the same level as the front. Essentially, this is the same technique we described in the bunny hop on page 108, just at higher speeds. The big difference is that the landing is critical. Try to land both wheels at the same time, or with the rear wheel landing marginally earlier. Never land with the front wheel first, as this just invites calamity.

Above: *You may never descend like this, but the techniques are the same.*

Above: *Your body position when descending at speed should involve fully extended but relaxed arms, and your body weight as far back as possible.*

Serious descending

More technical descents require a mixture of technique and bravery that only experience will bring to most mountain bikers. Determining what is rideable and what isn't is often as simple as making sure you have seen a more experienced rider get down a particular section in one piece.

We are not going to look at the techniques required to clear a section of trail as illustrated by the picture above – that is clearly the domain of the immensely talented and brave downhill crowd, and the nuances of their niche craft could generate an entire book. The aim here is to help you down sections you will find on established trails and routes, and that can be ridden on 'normal' mountain bikes.

First, let's look at body position: you want to keep your weight as far back as you safely can. Arms will be fully extended, but relaxed, with middle and ring fingers on the brake levers and a clenched thumb-and-first-finger grip around the bars. Generally, you will need to stand out of the saddle for the really steep stuff, and you will need to slide over the back of the saddle as far as you can to keep from toppling over forwards.

Using the front brake in these conditions can be tricky, but using the back brake can cause you to skid, so find a happy medium between the two. Once you have picked a line, and nine times out of ten the straightest line from top to bottom is the best, stick to it and let the bike roll as fast as you dare. Momentum is key – if you roll too slowly on the steep stuff, loose rocks and other impediments can bounce the front wheel off course

and make you tumble. If you do lose your line, stay calm and relaxed and rejoin it when you can.

Most steep descents like this have a run-off area at the bottom where the trail flattens out a bit, so keep your braking for when you are off the steep part and sort out speed and direction then. If you don't have the luxury of a run-off area, you will need to control both of these aspects on the steep section, and the key is to keep all braking and steering adjustments small and gradual. Generally, your momentum will do the job of getting you to the bottom of the hill – your job is to make sure you stay on top of the bike all the way down, and this is best achieved by letting it roll through any obstacles with a minimum of rider intervention. Watch more experienced riders and you realize that the ease with which they ride these sections is not bravado, but them letting the bike do its job and hanging on for the ride.

Over the edge

Drop-offs are amongst the most feared mountain bike obstacles, yet they are quite manageable once you have the basics. There are two distinct techniques, and the one you use will depend on both the height of the drop-off and the run-off area after it.

The first way to ride drop-offs will work for anything up to about a foot in height, and any drop-off where your chain ring clears the obstacle you are riding over. Roll towards the drop-off at walking pace and, as the front wheel rolls over it, shift your weight all the way over the back of the bike. As the back wheel rolls over and down, you can shift your weight forward again and carry on riding down the trail. This is an easy technique and one that, with practice, you'll be

Above: The most efficient drop-off technique is to wheelie off.

able to do at high speed and without thinking.

The second technique is more advanced, but will allow you to ride off higher steps and ledges. Basically, as the front wheel reaches the edge of the lip, pedal hard and pull up on the bars (essentially, you will be wheelie-ing off the edge) so that the front wheel keeps going at the height it was at when in contact with the ground. As the rear wheel travels over the lip, it will drop, and you can shift your weight back so that it touches the ground marginally before the front wheel does on the other, lower side of the step or drop-off. This technique takes a great deal of practice and is probably best learned on smaller drop-offs. Remember to compress your knees and elbows on landing to reduce the impact on you and the bike.

Above: Jumping – once you have seen that there is a safe place to land – is a good way of clearing drop-offs.

Storming singletrack

Much like climbing, descending on singletrack mountain bike trails requires plenty of forward planning and common sense. At its best, singletrack riding is exhilarating and fun, but the penalty for being over-ambitious is high. Although the speeds reached in these sections are comparatively low, the convenience of having a path through trees and rocks is limited by the fact that when you do lose the trail, you tend to hit something solid. Gear choice is a matter of personal preference, but look for one that is low enough to accelerate out of corners, but high enough that you can still wheelie when needed.

The first element of riding fast on singletrack is to look as far ahead as possible and plan. By the time your wheels are on a particular section of the trail, it is generally too late to react properly to changes in trail direction and surface, and crisis management at this point will mean you can't adequately plan for the next obstacle. By looking far enough ahead, you can spot changes and obstacles early enough to work out how best to deal with them, and how to deal with anything on the other side of them, creating an efficient flow that will make riding singletrack faster and safer.

If you are riding an event, make sure you are the first rider into any singletrack section. Not only will this make sure you stay ahead of

Above: *The key to riding fast on single-track is looking far ahead and planning.*

your opponents – there is simply no sensible way past on most singletrack – but it will also allow you to ride at your pace without being drawn into following somebody who is riding more slowly or quickly than your most comfortable, and safest, pace – following another rider tempts you to follow their example, and their mistakes.

The position on the bike for descending singletrack trails is a neutral one, preferably with the rider standing. Relaxed arms and legs will allow you to manoeuvre the bike using your body rather than the steering, allowing you to react to bumps, dips and obstacles with ease. Bar ends should be left well alone, as you will need to be

Above: *Provided that you plan your route in advance, you will find singletrack easy, and an enjoyable, exhilarating ride.*

riding with a finger on each brake to control your speed properly.

One of the major difficulties on singletrack is that ruts sometimes form in the path parallel to your direction of travel. This is due to either over-use and bad trail maintenance, or heavy rain washing down the trail. If you are stuck on one side of one of these ruts, and need to cross it, you should be able to do so by bunny hopping sideways. As before, the technique is to pull back and up on the bars, then lift your feet under you, just to introduce some sideways movement. If you are riding slowly, or are not confident enough to hop sideways, you can unclip one foot and use it as a pivot around which you can lift the front wheel and deposit it on the other side of the rut. The back wheel should follow happily.

Above: *Downhills such as this, amidst beautiful scenery, are enormous fun and can be attempted at a relatively low speed by the less adventurous.*

Right: *If your cross-country course has a section that is too technical, simply get off and walk. If you're feeling up to the challenge, try bunny hopping.*

Cornering

Cornering off-road is a skill in its own right, no matter what surface you are riding on or in what conditions. Stick to the three essential elements – plot a line, look where you want to go and brake before you turn – and you will survive even the tightest of turns.

The first stage of successful cornering is picking the most suitable line. The standard approach is to start wide, clip the apex of the bend and exit wide again. This will let you carry as much speed as possible out of the corner. On wide-open forest roads, this is a fine technique, but on more closed-in trails and roads, steer a little wide of the apex, allowing yourself a margin of error should there be rain ruts or unexpected obstacles in the path.

Next, focus on your brakes and your gears. All of your braking should be done before you start turning, so that you can concentrate on the exit of the corner. Braking in a straight line is also far safer, because a locked rear wheel will slide predictably, whereas skidding once you are in a corner can cause the back wheel to choose a different line to the one you planned. Use the front brake as

Above: Keep your body loose and your focus on the path ahead.
Left: Use one finger to brake and avoid skidding. The front brake should be used more than the rear for greater control.

much as you can, as it offers considerably more power and control as your weight shifts forward. Just take care on really steep downhills – the consequence of applying too much front brake can be embarrassing and painful.

Gearing is important too, as you will need to get up to race pace as quickly as possible after exiting the corner. Choose a gear that maximizes the speed out of the exit, and make sure you shift into it before you reach the corner, so that you can focus on the corner itself.

The third element of cornering sounds the simplest, but is the trickiest. Our nature is to look at the obstacle we want to steer around and try to avoid it. It is far better to look where you actually want to go and ignore the obstacle, as this will let you move your focus further through the corner whilst you rely on your perfectly picked line to keep you upright.

Berms are raised, sculpted sections of trail designed for maximum cornering fun. They are mostly found on BMX or four-cross tracks, but you will also find them in a smaller proportion on most off-road trails. The key to riding berms successfully is committing to the extra speed they will let you carry through the corner. Moderate your speed before entering the berm, enter as high as you can and keep as high as you can. Exit by dropping down the berm slightly, using it to slingshot you onto the next section of trail. Body position

Above: As you enter a berm, moderate your speed and trust to the extra speed the corner will give you. Enter high and stay high.

Above: Drop down the berm slightly and use the slope to slingshot you out of the corner. Always keep your body position central and relaxed.

on big berms is important - you can maximize your speed by keeping your body central and loose, your outside leg at the bottom of the pedalstroke and the bike leaning in to keep it perpendicular to the bank of the berm. On deep berms, you can pedal to keep your speed up, but be aware of how close to

the ground your pedal is so that you don't dig it into the ground and crash. Smaller berms and corrugations in the trail can be used, almost like a guide rail, to give you more traction through the corner, but be sure you know where the 'rail' ends before you get there so you can plan accordingly.

TRAINING

Training properly for mountain biking is a tough and time-consuming process, but well worth it if you want to get the most out of your sport. For some that might just mean losing a few pounds and increasing their ability to venture further into nature. For others it might be challenging for a regional or national title. No matter what your goal is, the basic principles will be the same: a plan, a lot of dedication and the ability to listen to your body and allow it to improve.

The first thing you need to do before starting any training programme is have a proper medical exam. Your physician will have a standard battery of tests that satisfy the criteria set by insurance companies, but if you have gone to the trouble of seeing a doctor in the first place, why not get your blood tested for nutritional deficiencies and imbalances at the same time? Many cases of 'overtraining' have been remedied not by reducing the amount of training time, but by identifying iron deficiencies and the like. Constructive training is a combination of breaking down and rebuilding your muscles, and it is vital to monitor this process as closely as you can. Recovery is almost more important than intense training and is what sets the full-time athletes apart from regular riders with full-time jobs and lives. Even with a full-time job and family, it is not difficult to match their 20–30 hours a week on the bike, but finding the time for an hour of massage and a few hours' sleep each afternoon, in addition to a full nine or ten hours' sleep at night, is not always possible.

Warming up and warming down properly will not only help you recover more quickly from intense rides, but also help you avoid injury. Cold muscles are prone to stretches and tears. Warming up can be as simple as riding gently for fifteen to twenty minutes before your intense efforts start, and can be supported by some very light stretching, as outlined on pages 40–41. Warming down involves a fifteen-minute spin session to loosen the legs followed by full stretching. Few of us bother with

Above: Group training can be a fun and sociable way of building your fitness.

stretching, and most of us get away with it purely because cycling is such a gentle sport in the first place.

Finally some advice that will sound strange at first: be prepared to ignore the training programmes you will find later in this section. Now I have your attention, the reason behind this suggestion is that there is a current trend towards personal coaching in cycling. Historically, only top-level riders have had personal coaches, and cyclists in general have been happy to self-coach using books and manuals and doses of common sense. Today, with the advent of ready access to the internet and downloadable training tools such as heart-rate monitors and power meters, it is possible to maintain a one-on-one coaching relationship with an expert across the world. This subjective outlook on your progress, or lack thereof, could just transform your training.

Above: Warming up properly with some light stretching will help to prevent muscles pulling and tearing.

Setting goals

One of the most difficult aspects of race training is setting goals and sticking to them. A five or six month training programme can make your ultimate goal seem a very, very long way away. As with any long journey, it makes sense to set out with a map, and identify points of reference along your way so that you can make sure you are on the right track.

The first important step is to write your stages down for the upcoming season and beyond – this turns them from good intentions into goals. Divide them into three distinct categories; world-renowned coach Joe Friel describes them best as A-races (plan to peak for these, including significant taper period), B-races (less important, minor

peak) and C-races (no reduction in training volume, use as one of your workouts).

Next, decide on a goal around which you want to build your season – your A-race. This could be an important local event, or a championship, or just a personal best time. Even if it seems as if your goal is minor, it is important to have one to work towards to keep yourself motivated. These goals should be as specific as possible, a series of minor performance-oriented goals culminating in one major outcome-based goal, say an event you plan to win, or a personal best in a given event. The danger with outcome-based goals is that they can have a negative effect if their narrow targets are not hit perfectly, so make sure they are realistic.

Above: *Using a heart-rate monitor is a good way of measuring progress.*

Don't limit your goals to the end of your current training cycle. Just as you get stronger and faster from training-block to training-block, your year-on-year improvement will allow you to set goals for two, three or even ten years down the road. Again, a distant goal is better than no goal at all, if only to keep you focused.

Which brings us to the next consideration: make sure all of your goals are achievable. There is no point in setting yourself the goal of winning your national cross-country championships if you are not one of the best riders in your region. Make sure you are realistic about your ultimate season goal, as well as

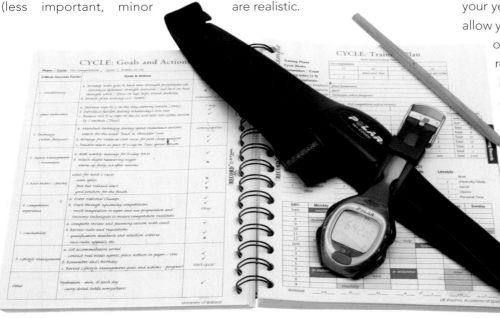

Above: *Writing your goals down in a training diary can be a great motivator – ticking them off and seeing how far you've progressed is a great feeling.*

Above: *Planning your season around a race is a great goal to set yourself. Working towards it will keep you motivated, but make sure it is a realistic, achievable aim.*

each of your intermediate goals. If you are in doubt, bounce your goals off friends and riding partners who know your abilities.

One of the keys to successfully setting goals is the ability to measure results. You can use either a heart-rate monitor or power meter to keep track of your training, but on race day, time is what absolutely counts. Create a test course and use circuits of it as part of your goal setting. Work out

what time you need to do it in to achieve your major season goal, and then set out a series of tests building through your training period to points at which you can properly assess your progress.

Write your goals down in your training diary, and keep referring back to them at the beginning of a training cycle, the beginning of a month or when you have a spare moment. The more you read your goals to yourself, the more

defined and less subject to vacillating levels of motivation they can be. Positive reinforcement like this will help them to become part of your subconscious, and hence more achievable.

Finally, remember that these are goals, not commandments. Your personal and work situations are guaranteed to change to some degree through the course of a long season, so be flexible and reasonable with your aspirations.

Planning your season

Planning your racing season properly starts with setting your goals, as we discussed on the previous pages. The ideal programme will take you through a 17-week cycle, divided into base, strength and peak-season training. For most riders, this is about as long as you can stay focused and motivated.

The base period is possibly the most important. A full eight weeks long, think of this period as the base of a pyramid, at the top of which is your A-race. The wider and stronger you make the base, the higher and more stable the peak will be.

The base period is where you will build your foundation for your season, and the emphasis is on long and slow. You will build your aerobic fitness as well as develop your muscles' efficiency to absorb oxygen. It is also an important phase in that it allows you to strengthen tendons and ligaments in anticipation of the harder work to come, helping you to avoid injury. Use these longer, less intense days in the saddle wisely; test new energy drinks and bars, play around with your position on the bike and perfect your pedal stroke.

The majority of your riding at this time is likely to be on the road, because riding off-road demands too much of the body, even on easier routes. The longer you can moderately train, the better you will race when that time comes.

Above: You will need to build your fitness as you work towards your main goal. Gradually reduce the time and distance you spend on the bike, concentrating on specific training.

Above: *Interval training is a great way of building strength and fitness. Cross-country racers should work on short, fast sessions that will quickly build up your fitness.*

Right: *Marathon and endurance racers should focus on doing longer rides, but be careful not to overtrain.*

The next phase is the strengthening phase. This is a four-week phase that will see a gradual reduction in overall time and distance on the bike, and a greater degree of specific training. You will start with interval training and, at this point, your choice of A-race will begin to determine your training schedule. Cross-country racers will focus on shorter, faster sessions, while marathon racers will need to build up to completing three-quarters of the full race distance a month before the big day.

The third phase is the peak-season section of your programme. This is also four weeks long, and sees a vast reduction in the quantity of your training, and a big increase in the quality. More and harder intervals and test races will help you to convert the past four months' work into results at your chosen race, but you will need to make sure you allow for adequate recovery. Overtraining is very easy at this stage, as it is easy to feel you are not doing enough because the number of hours you spend on the bike has dropped so dramatically. You will need every second of rest you can get at this point, however, as the increased intensity will drain you both physically and mentally.

The end of the peak-season needs to taper to your big race. It is generally accepted that hard training efforts within ten days of your race will result in you being more fatigued than strengthened, so focus on radically shorter rides that check your equipment is in perfect working order and on rest, recovery, nutrition and hydration. Just remember not to do anything outside your normal routine: don't suddenly eat ten bowls of pasta a day because you need the carbohydrates. At this point your body should be at its leanest and fittest, and this can often leave you susceptible to picking up colds, so avoid sufferers if possible.

Above: *Choose a heart-rate monitor with a coded chest strap – otherwise you may pick up the readings of other riders.*

Above: *The more advanced pulse monitors are well worth investing in – their added features make it worthwhile.*

Monitoring your training

The most convenient and cost-effective way to monitor your training is to use a heart-rate monitor. These are widely available, in a range of price points and sophistication levels. On a basic level, the simplest unit will tell you exactly what you need to know – your heart rate. But, given the enormous amount of information and feedback it will give you, it is advisable not to scrimp when looking to buy one of these gadgets. They can seem expensive and look complicated, but they are usually more intuitive than they first seem, and you will be able to justify the extra cost comfortably at the end of a successful season.

The first consideration when buying a monitor is to look for a reputable brand. This is important as electronic equipment is susceptible to glitches, and the bigger names will have exemplary warranties and guarantees should anything go wrong.

Secondly, look for a unit that has a coded chest strap. This will ensure that you pick up your own heart rate and only yours, a vital feature in training groups or races where your unit will be close enough to read off your neighbour's chest-strap.

Next, if you are bothering to buy yourself a heart-rate monitor, it makes sense to get one that records your workouts and allows you to download them to your computer. This doubles the functionality of the tool: not only are you able to monitor yourself instantaneously on the bike, but you are able to analyze what you got right and what you got wrong afterwards. The former is key to making sure you ride the hard stuff hard enough, and the latter will help you monitor recovery and efficiency, and avoid burnout and overtraining.

Out on the road, target-zone alarms will help immensely with your training: you will know when you are riding with the necessary intensity, without having to look down and read off numbers. Where they really come into their own is during the base phase and on recovery rides. Out on a trail, riding with your buddies, it is easy to ignore a dial that tells you that you are a few beats over the 120 that is your recovery limit. An audible, insistent alarm will be harder to ignore.

To use your new monitor properly, you need to know what your maximum heart rate is. The old rule of thumb, the one that says 220 minus your age is a good approximation, is virtually useless: many top-level riders have maximum heart rates of over 200, yet there is a recorded case of a top European road professional who could only get up into the 170s. Everybody is different, and the only way to find out your maximum is to get on the bike.

Start by finding a traffic-free 10 km (6 mile) stretch of flat or slightly uphill road, with no traffic lights, stop signs or roundabouts. After a 15 minute warm-up, ride at a medium pace, with a cadence of about 80. Shift into your next biggest gear, maintaining the same cadence, and stay there for two minutes, before shifting into the next gear. Repeat this until you cannot pedal another stroke, and then stand up and sprint for 200 m (656 ft). Your heart rate at the end of this effort will be as close to your maximum as it is recommended to be.

Convention takes this maximum rate and uses it to set training zones, with your training heart rate as a percentage of your maximum, in the table below. These zones will be used in the training guides later in this section.

One of the most useful functions of measuring your heart rate is as a check on your recovery rate and general health. Take your pulse every morning, just after you wake up. This resting pulse should gradually get lower as you get fitter – top-level riders can get as low as 36 or 37 beats per minute – and it

Above: *Heart-rate monitors can help to ensure that you don't overtrain.*

can be a valuable early warning sign of overtraining. An increase of more than five beats per minute, more than two mornings in a row, is an indication that you should roll over and go back to sleep. Your body is telling you that you need more rest. Don't, however, overreact to one anomalous reading – it may just be due to a bad dream, some caffeine still in your system or waking up suddenly.

TRAINING ZONES

Zone 1	60–65%	Easy riding, recovery
Zone 2	65–70%	Base training
Zone 3	70–80%	Aerobic capacity training
Zone 4	80–85%	Lactate threshold training
Zone 5	>85%	VO_2 max training

Above: The Polar unit has a reputation for being hard to set up, but it is good value for money and can be transferred to different bikes with ease.

Power meters

Much as heart-rate training transformed cycling in the early 90s, the professional peloton has whole-heartedly embraced the use of power meters. And for very good reason: ultimately, no matter what the revs of your engine are, it is how much power you can transfer into forward momentum that determines your success as a cyclist.

There are three major units that measure your power output on the bike: the SRM unit, which is housed in a dedicated crankset; the Powertap hubset, which requires you to have a dedicated wheel built; and the Polar power add-on for S-series heart-rate monitors. All three give you heart rate and normal cycle-computer readings such as speed, time and distance, and download to a computer for workout review.

For the mountain biker, the Powertap system is probably the best bet, as its price tag makes it possible to have both on- and off-road wheels, should you want to measure your output on all surfaces. The SRM costs four times as much as the Powertap, and is available in a triple chain-ring configuration for the mountain bike, but most off-roaders spend the majority of their training miles on the road, so you will have to make a decision about where you are most likely to want to get your feedback. The Polar system relies on changes in chain tension to

Above: The Powertap system is probably the most accurate and is very easy to calibrate – it will only need to be zeroed every two weeks.

measure your output, and has received a mixed response from riders. It is fiddly to set up, but has the advantage that it can be transferred from bike to bike, and is the cheapest of the three. As to which is most accurate, Powertap lays claim to the greatest accuracy, with SRM slightly less so, and Polar marginally more difficult to get consistent readings from.

The Powertap is very easy to calibrate – you need to tell the unit when you are producing zero watts so that it can accurately convert your power input into a wattage – and only needs to be zeroed every fortnight or so. The SRM requires zeroing every time you ride, as does the Polar unit. This process is a simple one – freewheel and press a couple of buttons – but critical to the accuracy of your training with power.

Training with a power meter is similar in principle to using a heart-rate monitor: find your maximum power, work out your training zones and create a programme accordingly. Determining your maximum power is more difficult than finding your maximum heart rate, and generally requires you to visit a university research department or cycling-specific gym. It involves a ramp test, for which you start riding, after a warm-up, at a nominal wattage (normally your body weight, in kilograms, multiplied by four). This is then increased by 25 watts every two and a half minutes until you

Above: *Although the SRM crank system is the most expensive option, it will help you to monitor your training accurately.*

can pedal no more. This normally works out to be somewhere between ten and fifteen minutes of gruelling pedalling, but will give you a value on which to base your power workouts. It is possible to perform this test yourself, on an indoor trainer, but it will always be more accurate in a laboratory situation, with a professional trainer managing the test.

For the purposes of this book, we have used heart rate as the basis of the training programmes laid out in this chapter. Heart-rate monitors are less expensive, more versatile and easier for the layman to use. You can estimate heart rate zones and be relatively inaccurate in doing so without losing too much in the way of training results. Power-based training is trickier in

that, to get the most out of it, you will need to concentrate much harder on the numbers. An error of 5 per cent in judging a heart-rate zone will probably do you little harm – it may not be optimal, but no damage is likely to be done – but to be 5 per cent out of a power zone is risky. The advantage of training with power is that when the zones are correct, your return, in race performance, is far higher and more controllable.

Because training with power is so much more of an exact science, it is probably best to consult with an experienced coach, rather than set a programme yourself. It may cost you a bit more money than trying to do it yourself, but the difference in your results will be well worth the extra expense.

Strength training

Strength training is an often-overlooked part of even the most experienced cyclist's training regimen. The general feeling seems to be that building your strength on the bike is more beneficial than sweating it out in a gym, but in truth, a sensible weights routine will help you to not only grow stronger, but also to avoid fatigue. This is particularly the case for mountain bikers, where the variety of terrain and surfaces force riders to utilize their upper body muscles more than road cyclists.

The best time to do your strength training is through your off-season—winter in most cycling communities. Working out in the weights room can leave you feeling sluggish and slow, so make sure you taper it off to the bare minimum when you are getting into the early-season and peak-season phases of your training.

Before you hit the gym make sure you are kitted out with snug-fitting clothing that won't catch on equipment and a pair of dedicated gym shoes. A proper warm-up, either on your bike or on an indoor cycle at the gym, is vital in combating injuries, so factor in twenty minutes of light cardiovascular work before you start lifting.

The key to getting the most out of your weight training is holding your form and knowing your limits. If you are lifting to gain strength, you will be using heavier weights but lifting them for between five and ten repetitions. For building muscle endurance, a lighter weight lifted 15 to 20 times will do the trick. In both cases, the aim is to keep all your movements slow and controlled. The moment you need to jerk or rush a movement, you are either lifting too much or fatigued. Either reduce the weight or finish there and move on to the next exercise.

Aim to do three sessions a week, each running to about an hour. Any longer or more frequent than this and you run the risk of becoming a weightlifter who mountain bikes, rather than the other way round. You should be able to include six to ten sets in an hour-long session, and it is important not to work the same muscles two sessions in a row. Try to schedule one of three groups each session: for example, legs on a Monday, arms on a Wednesday and back, chest and abs on a Friday. You should also look to group muscles that oppose each other in the same workout to avoid imbalances. If you build up the pulling muscle (biceps) more than the pushing one (triceps) you run the risk of strains and possibly more serious injuries.

Finally, a decent warm-down and stretching routine will be the final link in the chain, helping you to avoid injury and increase suppleness.

Above: *With knees bent at around 90 degrees, gradually straighten your legs.*

Above: *Extend your legs until they are almost straight, then bend them again.*

LEG PRESS ▲

Works your quadriceps

Use a dedicated leg-press machine for this, rather than the traditional free-standing squat, which puts undue strain on your knees. Start with your knees bent to about 90 degrees, upper body relaxed, and gradually straighten by pushing against the foot plate until your legs are almost fully extended. Make sure your grip on the side handles is loose. Slowly return to your start position.

LEG CURL ▶

Works your thigh muscles and hamstrings

Start with your knees bent at 90 degrees, the end of the bench about an inch behind them, and the lifting pads just above your ankles. Slowly straighten your legs, stopping just before they are fully extended, then slowly return to your start position. Hamstrings are generally underdeveloped in cyclists, so choose very light weights and build up slowly.

Above: With knees bent and arms loosely on the handles, slowly straighten your legs as far as you can without fully extending.

Above: Once extended, return to the start position. Be careful not to add too many weights – build up slowly.

CALF RAISE ▶

Works your calves

With your feet about the same width apart as on a bike, stand on a raised step with your heels lowered and holding a barbell on your shoulders, behind your neck. Tuck your shoulders under the weights and lift your heels up, slowly extending as high as you can. Pause at the top and lower slowly.

Right: Standing on a raised step, lower your heels over the edge with a barbell balanced comfortably on your shoulders. Lift your heels up until you can extend no further, then slowly lower them back to your starting position.

Left: Lie with your arms crossed and feet flat on the floor.

Left: Lift your torso, keeping your lower back on the ground.

Above: Stand with feet shoulder-width apart.

Above: Keep your back bent while lifting the barbell.

BENT-OVER ROW ▲

Works lower back and upper arms

Stand with your feet shoulder-width apart. Bending from your waist, with your knees slightly bent, pick up a barbell, palms downwards and hands the same width as your handlebars. Lift straight towards the ceiling until it touches your chest, keeping your back and legs in the same position.

CRUNCH ▲

Works abdominal muscles

Lie on your back, knees at about 45 degrees, feet slightly apart. Cross your arms on your chest and slowly lift your torso towards your knees, keeping your lower back on the ground. When your abdominal muscles start to feel the strain, hold for a second, and relax back to the ground. Repeat without break and without rushing.

Above: Start with your neck and back fully straight.

Above: Slowly bend over, keeping your back extended.

Above: Keep your arms straight and palms forward.

Above: Raise the bar, keeping your elbows tucked in.

BACK EXTENSION ▲

Works your lower back muscles

With your hips just over the edge of the bench, your ankles snug in the padded bars and your fingers touching your head, slowly bend over, keeping your neck and upper back straight. Do no more than three sets of twenty of these, as your lower back is susceptible to injury.

BARBELL CURL ▲

Works your biceps

Hold the barbell in front of your body, arms straight down and palms forwards. Slowly raise the bar, keeping your back and neck straight and elbows to your side, until the bar almost touches your collarbone, then drop slowly back to the starting position.

Above: Hold the dumbbell to your side, palm inwards.

Above: Straighten your arm, raising the dumbbell.

TRICEPS LUNGE ▲

Works your triceps

With a dumbbell in your right hand, palm inwards, lower arm vertical, upper arm horizontal and elbow at your side, put your left knee and hand on a bench. Straighten your right arm behind you, parallel to the ground, then return it to the starting position.

Above: Keep your feet flat on the floor and slightly apart.

Above: Make sure your back stays flat against the bench.

BENCH PRESS ▲

Works your chest and upper arms

Grip the barbell with your hands shoulder-width apart and directly above your chest. Your feet should be flat on the ground, slightly apart, and knees bent to 90 degrees. Without arching your back, lift the bar off its rests, lower to your chest at nipple level and raise again. Don't use momentum and bounce off your chest, but move slowly for best results.

Above: Keep your hands quite close together on the bar.

Above: Lift the bar straight up, keeping your back straight.

UPRIGHT ROW ▲

Works the trapezius muscles and the rest of your shoulders

With a narrow grip on a barbell, arms hanging down in front of you and palms inwards, lift the bar straight up until it is at nipple level. Hold for two seconds then slowly drop. The bar must only move straight up or down, no backwards or forwards motion.

Above: 'Shrug' your shoulders, then roll them back and forth.

SHRUG ◀

Works your neck and shoulder muscles

Start in the same position as the upright row, but with your hands shoulder-width apart. Keeping your arms straight, lift the bar towards your head, and when you can 'shrug' no higher, roll your shoulders slowly forwards and then backwards. Slowly drop your shoulders back down to their original position.

Stretching

Stretching after training, either in the gym or on the bike, will help relax tired muscles and accelerate the recovery process. Stretching also increases flexibility and suppleness, which in turn help avoid injury and allow your muscles to perform at a higher level of efficiency in more extreme conditions.

Until fairly recently it was accepted practice to stretch before and after exercise, but studies have shown that pre-event stretching can actually cause injury instead of preventing it, as stretching cold muscles can cause strains and tears. Rather limit your stretching to post-ride as part of your recovery routine, when your muscles are warm and at their most supple.

Never bounce when you stretch. All movements should be gradual and you should never feel pain whilst stretching. Stop and hold your position for about 20 seconds when you feel tightness in the muscles, then relax and repeat two more times.

Once you have become accustomed to stretching, you can start to expand your routine to non-riding days too, and even stretch in between sets in the gym.

Left: Lie face-down on the floor with arms and legs fully stretched out.

Left: Raise your legs, shoulders, head and arms and balance for a few seconds.

ABDOMINALS AND LOWER BACK ▲

Lie on the floor, stomach and hips down, looking ahead of you with arms held straight in front of you. Lift your head, legs, shoulders and arms so that only your hips and abdomen are touching the ground. Hold, and then slowly lower to the floor again.

Left: Stretch out your legs and point your toes, holding your arms above your head.

Left: Move your arms over your head until they touch the floor, then raise them again.

LYING EXTENSION ▲

On your back, straighten your legs and point your toes. Lace your fingers, palms upwards, and straighten your arms towards the ceiling. Slowly rotate them over your head until they touch the ground, and slowly raise them to the original position.

Above: Bend your knees and keep hands under shoulders.

Above: Roll your body back over your feet.

BACK AND SIDES ▲

Get on your hands and knees, hands directly under shoulders and knees bent to 90 degrees. Keep your hands in the same place, but roll your body back until you are sitting on your feet, then slowly roll back up again.

Above: Keep your back straight.

Above: Raise your arms.

CHEST STRETCH ▲

Stand up straight, feet slightly apart and back straight. Lace your fingers behind your back, arms straight and palms inwards. Without bending your back, extend your arms backwards and upwards.

Above: Grip your ankles with your hands.

Above: Press down with your elbows and feel the stretch.

GROIN ▲

Sitting with a straight back and neck, put your feet sole-to-sole, hands gripping your ankles, and elbows resting on the inside of your knees. Gently press downwards with the elbows until you feel tightness in your inner thighs.

HIPS ◄

Sit on the floor and tuck the left foot under the right buttock. Place your right foot on the outside of your left knee and gently pull your right knee towards your chest, keeping your back straight. Change legs and repeat.

QUADS ▲

Standing up straight with something to steady yourself on, grab your left ankle with your left hand and tuck it behind your buttock. As you gently pull your foot towards your bottom, feel the stretch in your quads.

CALVES ▲

Stand on a step or a pavement. Put the toes of one foot on the edge of the step and drop the heel down below the level of the toes until you feel the stretch in your calf muscles.

Recovery

The most overlooked part of most mountain bikers' training programmes is recovery. It is all well and good to put in the required number of hours on the bike and complete the full repertoire of intervals you have planned for your first hard session of the week – this is what we are here to do, after all, to train hard, break down muscle fibres and get stronger in the process. But how often do we go straight to work after a morning ride and wonder why we feel so sore the next morning, or get back late from an evening hill-climbing session and rush straight out for some drinks before a late dinner and blame the third glass of wine for our aching body the next day?

The most important piece of the recovery puzzle is nutrition. It is thought you have a two hour window to maximize your fluid and glycogen replenishment. In this short period after a training session, your weary body is more

Above: Eight hours of sleep a night is needed by most adults, but you will need to try and add an hour for every hour you train.

receptive to water and energy replacements than at any other time, so concentrate on ingesting one litre of water, depending on how long your ride was, and a minimum of 70 grams of carbohydrate – an energy bar or a couple of bananas – within the first

hour. The easiest way of doing this is through a proper recovery drink, which may also contain some protein and vitamins and minerals. Next, aim to eat a proper meal, with a balance between fat, protein and carbohydrates and plenty of vegetables or fruit to replenish lost minerals.

Stretching, as discussed on the previous pages, is also a key factor in recovery, and should be done religiously after every ride and gym session. Once you have a stretching routine you should only need to take 15–20 minutes over it, so it can be easily fitted into your routine.

Massage is the big secret that the professionals willingly share with us, but that few of us have the time, or money, to utilize properly. The top-level riders spend a minimum of an

Right: Nutrition is vital for cyclists in training – bananas are a great source of carbohydrate and will provide energy both before and after your ride.

Above: *If you don't relish the idea of having a completely bike-free day, a gentle recovery ride can do a lot of good. Be careful not to raise your heart rate and you will aid your body's break down of lactic acid.*

hour on a masseur's table after every ride, and research indicates that regular massage can cut your recovery time in half. For the serious amateur rider, a weekly massage, maybe at the start of the week to get you lithe and relaxed, will probably do the trick. Just be warned – this is no relaxing back rub. The whole idea of sports massage is to break up the clumps of lactic acid and tight spots in your muscles and work them out of your system. This process can be painful, but it really does help.

Sleep is also a precious commodity for cyclists-in-training. As a rule of thumb, a normal adult needs about eight hours of sleep a day. Use a guideline of an extra hour for every hour you train, and you can see how difficult it is to get enough sleep and balance a working and family life. This is where the dedication of a successful cyclist comes into play. It is not just getting up at six in the morning to ride that requires discipline; getting to bed by nine in the evening, when your friends are out on the town, perhaps takes greater discipline.

Rest days, for many riders, are strictly bike-free days – the author has not trained on a Monday since 1985 – and that works well for some. But if you simply can't go a day without riding, an active recovery ride can be as beneficial as sitting at home. Keep your heart rate below 50 per cent of your maximum and the marginally increased circulation will help the body break down lactic acid.

Recovery should also be an integral part of your training programme. Leave one week after each block of four as a lower mileage and recovery week, with a few days of recovery rides included. It will give your body, and your mind, a chance to rest and relax, and let you train much harder in the next four-week cycle.

Above: The first stages of the training programme will establish an endurance base on which to build.

Training programmes

WEEKS 1–8

The emphasis through the eight weeks of base training is on high mileage and low intensity. We will not ignore intensity totally; the occasional bursts of speed are necessary for most riders to refresh their legs and also to remind them why they are doing all this training in the first place – to get fitter, to get faster and to achieve their training goals.

These programmes have been compiled to help beginner, intermediate and keen mountain bikers work their way to their chosen target for the year. The beginner will be ready, after the 17 weeks is up, to tackle a two-hour duration mountain bike race; the intermediate a three-hour short marathon event or a fast cross-country event; and the expert a full marathon off-road event, where finishing times can range from four to seven hours.

These programmes use the heart-rate zones laid out on page 133 of this book. For your health and safety, consult a medical doctor and have a full check-up before you start this or any other programme. And note that this is an average guide for three average cyclists. Few of us are average, so be sensible and if your body is telling you that you are doing too much or too little, adjust accordingly and gradually. Training will, at times, be both uncomfortable and tedious. If it remains either for more than a few days, adjust as much as you wish

For both zone 1 and zone 2, keep in a light gear and keep your cadence high, between 90 and 100. For now, keep your rides on the flats. There will be plenty of hill work in later stages.

Week 1	Beginner	Intermediate	Experienced
Monday	Rest	Rest	Rest
Tuesday	30 mins zone 1	45 mins zone 1	1 hr zone 1
Wednesday	Rest	1 hr zone 1	1 hr zone 1
Thursday	45 mins zone 1	45 mins zone 1	1 hr zone 1
Friday	Rest	Rest	Rest
Saturday	1 hr zone 1	2 hrs zone 1	2 hrs zone 1
Sunday	1 hr zone 1	2 hrs zone 1	2 hrs zone 1

Week 5	Beginner	Intermediate	Experienced
Monday	Rest	Rest	Rest
Tuesday	45 mins zone 1	1 hr zone 1	1 hr zone 1
Wednesday	Rest	$1\frac{1}{2}$ hrs zone 1/2	$2\frac{1}{2}$ hrs zone 1/2
Thursday	45 mins zone 1	1 hr zone 1	1 hr zone 1
Friday	Rest	Rest	Rest
Saturday	2 hrs zone 1/2	2 hrs zone 1/2	3 hrs zone 1/2
Sunday	1 hr zone 1	2 hrs zone 1/2	$2\frac{1}{2}$ hrs zone 1/2

Week 2	Beginner	Intermediate	Experienced
Monday	Rest	Rest	Rest
Tuesday	45 mins zone 1	1 hr zone 1	1 hr zone 1
Wednesday	Rest	1 hr zone 1	2 hrs zone 1
Thursday	1 hr zone 1	1 hr zone 1	1 hr zone 1
Friday	Rest	Rest	Rest
Saturday	$1\frac{1}{4}$ hrs zone 1	2 hrs zone 1	2 hrs zone 1
Sunday	1 hr zone 1	2 hrs zone 1	2 hrs zone 1

Week 6	Beginner	Intermediate	Experienced
Monday	Rest	Rest	Rest
Tuesday	1 hr zone 1	1 hr zone 1	1 hr zone 1/2
Wednesday	Rest	2 hrs zone 1/2	$2\frac{1}{2}$ hrs zone 1
Thursday	1 hr zone 1	1 hr zone 1	1 hr zone 1
Friday	Rest	Rest	Rest
Saturday	2 hrs zone 1/2	3 hrs zone 1/2	$3\frac{1}{2}$ hrs zone 1/2
Sunday	$1\frac{1}{2}$ hrs zone 1	2 hrs zone 1/2	$2\frac{1}{2}$ hrs zone 1/2

Week 3	Beginner	Intermediate	Experienced
Monday	Rest	Rest	Rest
Tuesday	45 mins zone 1	1 hr zone 1	1 hr zone 1
Wednesday	Rest	$1\frac{1}{2}$ hrs zone 1	$2\frac{1}{2}$ hrs zone 1
Thursday	$1\frac{1}{4}$ hrs zone 1	1 hr zone 1	1 hr zone 1
Friday	Rest	Rest	Rest
Saturday	$1\frac{1}{2}$ hrs zone 1	3 hrs zone 1	3 hrs zone 1
Sunday	1 hr zone 1	3 hrs zone 1	3 hrs zone 1

Week 7	Beginner	Intermediate	Experienced
Monday	Rest	Rest	Rest
Tuesday	1 hr zone 1	1 hr zone 1	2 hrs zone 1
Wednesday	Rest	$2\frac{1}{2}$ hrs zone 2	3 hrs zone 2
Thursday	1 hr zone 2	$1\frac{1}{2}$ hrs zone 2	2 hrs zone 2
Friday	Rest	Rest	Rest
Saturday	1 hr zone 2	$3\frac{1}{2}$ hrs zone 2	4 hrs zone 2
Sunday	1 hr zone 2	$2\frac{1}{2}$ hrs zone 2	3 hrs zone 2

Week 4	Beginner	Intermediate	Experienced
Monday	Rest	Rest	Rest
Tuesday	45 mins zone 1	1 hr zone 1	1 hr zone 1
Wednesday	Rest	1 hr zone 1	$1\frac{1}{2}$ hrs zone 1
Thursday	45 mins zone 1	1 hr zone 1	1 hr zone 1
Friday	Rest	Rest	Rest
Saturday	1 hr zone 1	2 hrs zone 1	2 hrs zone 1
Sunday	1 hr zone 1	2 hrs zone 1	2 hrs zone 1

Week 8	Beginner	Intermediate	Experienced
Monday	Rest	Rest	Rest
Tuesday	45 mins zone 1	1 hr zone 1	1 hr zone 1
Wednesday	Rest	Rest	Rest
Thursday	45 mins zone 1	1 hr zone 1	1 hr zone 1
Friday	Rest	Rest	Rest
Saturday	1 hr zone 1	2 hrs zone 1	2 hrs zone 1
Sunday	1 hr zone 1	2 hrs zone 1	2 hrs zone 1

Above: Weeks nine to twelve of the training programme will build on your power and strength.

Training programmes

WEEKS 9–12

Now that we have the long, soul-searching base period under our belt, and our bodies are fit and prepared, we can delve into some sessions that will turn the large endurance base we have built into power and strength.

The majority of these sessions will still be ridden in zone 2, so that we can continue to build stamina and endurance, but you will see that there are some that call for zone 2/3. On these rides, the idea is to keep in the upper end of zone 2 (70 per cent of your maximum heart rate) on the flats, and push into zone 3 on the climbs. Up to now, all of our zone 1 and 2 riding has been done at a high cadence (90–100) in a light gear, but for these zone 3 sections, use a larger gear, stay seated and keep the cadence down to the 70–75 range. This will help develop leg strength.

Thursdays, in this period, see the introduction of intervals into our training programme. We will focus on long power intervals in this cycle, with shorter, more intense intervals in weeks 13 to 16, as race day draws near.

After a good warm-up (at least ten minutes) ride at 80 per cent of your maximum for six minutes, keeping cadence between 70 and 80. You can do this on a slight uphill, but not too steep. The rest period before you repeat the six minute interval is three minutes. Beginner riders start with three repeats in week nine, four in week ten and five in week eleven. Intermediate riders can look forward to four, five and six repeats, and the experts five, seven and nine repeats. Keep an eye on your form in these intervals: your pedalling should be controlled and powerful – no stamping.

Week 9	Beginner	Intermediate	Experienced	Week 11	Beginner	Intermediate	Experienced
Monday	Rest	Rest	Rest	Monday	Rest	Rest	Rest
Tuesday	45 mins zone 1	$1\frac{1}{2}$ hrs zone 1	2 hrs zone 2	Tuesday	1 hr zone 1	2 hrs zone 2	3 hrs zone 2
Wednesday	rest	2 hrs zone 2/3	3 hrs zone 2/3	Wednesday	Rest	$2\frac{1}{2}$ hrs zone 2/3	3 hrs zone 2/3
Thursday	1 hr zone 3/4	2 hrs zone 3/4	2 hrs zone 3/4	Thursday	1 hr zone 3/4	1 hr zone 3/4	$1\frac{1}{2}$ hrs zone 3/4
Friday	Rest	Rest	Rest	Friday	Rest	Rest	Rest
Saturday	$1\frac{1}{4}$ hrs zone 2/3	3 hrs zone 2/3	4 hrs zone 2/3	Saturday	$1\frac{3}{4}$ hrs zone 2/3	4 hrs zone 2/3	5 hrs zone 2/3
Sunday	1 hr zone 2	2 hrs zone 2	3 hrs zone 2	Sunday	$1\frac{1}{2}$ hrs zone 2	3 hrs zone 2	4 hrs zone 2

Week 10	Beginner	Intermediate	Experienced	Week 12	Beginner	Intermediate	Experienced
Monday	Rest	Rest	Rest	Monday	Rest	Rest	Rest
Tuesday	45 mins zone 1	1 hr zone 1	$2\frac{1}{2}$ hrs zone 2	Tuesday	45 mins zone 1	1 hr zone 1	1 hr zone 1
Wednesday	Rest	2 hrs zone 2/3	3 hrs zone 2/3	Wednesday	Rest	Rest	Rest
Thursday	1 hr zone 3/4	2 hrs zone 3/4	$2\frac{1}{2}$ hrs zone 3/4	Thursday	45 mins zone 1	1 hr zone 1	1 hr zone 1
Friday	Rest	Rest	Rest	Friday	Rest	Rest	Rest
Saturday	$1\frac{1}{2}$ hrs zone 2/3	$3\frac{1}{2}$ hrs zone 2/3	$4\frac{1}{2}$ hrs zone 2/3	Saturday	1 hr zone 1	2 hrs zone 1	2 hrs zone 1
Sunday	$1\frac{1}{4}$ hrs zone 2	3 hrs zone 2	$3\frac{1}{2}$ hrs zone 2	Sunday	1 hr zone 1	2 hrs zone 1	2 hrs zone 1

Right: *Remember to incorporate a gentle warm-up ride into your training days.*

Far right: *On harder rides, make sure you are pedalling smoothly, not stamping on the pedals.*

Training programmes
WEEKS 13–15

We are now in the final training phase and the hardest three weeks of the programme. Weekend rides are longer, with Saturday a race or a hard group ride with some sprints and surges to get your heart rate up, and Sunday a slower, more controlled effort. Mondays and Friday are still rest days, which you will need. If you want to take in an hour-long sub-50 per cent recovery ride on these days, it will do you good, but make sure it is below 50 per cent. Nutrition and recovery are critical in these weeks, as you will not have time to recover from any illness or overtraining before your goal event, and your body will be under a huge amount of strain in the lead up to the main event.

Tuesday is long interval day, a repeat of the intervals we did in weeks 9, 10 and 11, and Wednesday is a tempo ride at the upper reaches of zone 3, making sure there are few surges, sprints and changes in pace.

Thursdays become short interval days. For beginners, after a decent warm-up, ride in zone 4, at a cadence of 80–90, for two minutes. Rest for three minutes by riding in zone 1. If possible, avoid doing this on steep hills for now and increase this in week 13, with 5 repetitions, to 7 and 9 repetitions in weeks 14 and 15.

Below: An hour-long recovery ride will supplement your training, provided you keep effort below 50 per cent.

Week 13	Beginner	Intermediate	Experienced
Monday	Rest	Rest	Rest
Tuesday	1 hr zone 3/4	2 hrs zone 3/4	2 hrs zone 3/4
Wednesday	1 hr zone 3	2 hrs zone 3	2 hrs zone 3
Thursday	1 hr zone 3/4	2 hrs zone 3/4	2 hrs zone 3/4
Friday	Rest	Rest	Rest
Saturday	1 hr zone 2/3	3½ hrs zone 2/3	5 hrs zone 2/3
Sunday	1 hr zone 2	2½ hrs zone 2	4 hrs zone 2

Week 14	Beginner	Intermediate	Experienced
Monday	Rest	Rest	Rest
Tuesday	1¼ hrs zone 3/4	2 hrs zone 3/4	2 hrs zone 3/4
Wednesday	1 hr zone 3	2 hrs zone 3	3 hrs zone 3
Thursday	1 hr zone 3/4	2 hrs zone 3/4	2 hrs zone 3/4
Friday	Rest	Rest	Rest
Saturday	2 hrs zone 2/3	4 hrs zone 2/3	5½ hrs zone 1
Sunday	2 hrs zone 2	3 hrs zone 2	4½ hrs zone 1

Week 15	Beginner	Intermediate	Experienced
Monday	Rest	Rest	Rest
Tuesday	1¼ hrs zone 3/4	2 hrs zone 3/4	2 hrs zone 3/4
Wednesday	1 hr zone 3	2 hrs zone 3	3 hrs zone 3
Thursday	1 hr zone 3/4	2 hrs zone 3/4	2 hrs zone 3/4
Friday	Rest	Rest	Rest
Saturday	2¼ hrs zone 2/3	4½ hrs zone 2/3	6 hrs zone 2/3
Sunday	2½ hrs zone 2	3½ hrs zone 2	5 hrs zone 2

Intermediate riders will do three minute hard sessions, with a three minute recovery, repeated five, seven and nine times over the same three weeks. The expert riders will also do three-minute-hard followed by three-minute-rest cycles, but repeated six, nine and twelve times respectively.

Right and above:

Weeks 13–15 are the hardest phase of the programme. Look after your body during this period, as it will be under a lot of strain.

Training programmes
WEEKS 16–17

The final two weeks of this 17 week cycle are the tapering period that will take the progressive overload that we have subjected your body to and turn it into raw speed. Tapering is all about making sure the body has enough chance to recuperate fully before the event, but is a delicate balancing act as you want to keep your muscles used to the idea of working hard. If you simply took two weeks off the bike, you would lose fitness and feel sluggish and slow on race day. By tapering properly, and slotting in some short, fast efforts, you will hit the start line raring to go.

Week 16 sees a dramatic decrease in the length of rides, but you will still do short intervals on Tuesday, and a tempo at zone 3 on Wednesday, the last hard ride before race day. Saturday and Sunday should be relaxing rides where you can check your equipment and enjoy riding for the sake of riding, instead of

Below: This phase of the training programme involves short, fast rides that will hopefully set you up perfectly for your race. Longer rides follow, with the last hard ride completed several days before the big race, and plenty of rest days incorporated into your schedule.

Above: Your body will have recovered in the tapering period before your race.

Week 16	Beginner	Intermediate	Experienced	Week 17	Beginner	Intermediate	Experienced
Monday	Rest	Rest	Rest	Monday	30 min zone 2	30 min zone 1	30 min zone 1
Tuesday	1 hr zone 3/4	1 hr zone 3/4	2 hrs zone 3/4	Tuesday	Rest	Rest	Rest
Wednesday	Rest	Rest	2 hrs zone 2	Wednesday	30 min zone 2	1 hr zone 2	1 hr zone 2
Thursday	1 hr zone 3	1½ hr zone 3	2 hrs zone 3/4	Thursday	Rest	Rest	Rest
Friday	Rest	Rest	Rest	Friday	Rest	Rest	Rest
Saturday	1 hr zone 2/3	2 hrs zone 2/3	2 hrs zone 2/3	Saturday	30 min zone 2	30 min zone 2	30 min zone 2
Sunday	1 hr zone 2	2 hrs zone 2	2 hrs zone 2	Sunday	RACE DAY	RACE DAY	RACE DAY

focusing on your one goal. You have done all your hard work, and realistically you can improve no more by race day. You can, however ruin it all by riding too hard on either of these days, so resist temptation and save yourself for race day.

The final week is almost a complete week of rest. Monday is a very short recovery ride to keep the legs turning, and Wednesday and Saturday are slightly longer rides – but short compared to anything the last three months has seen – with half a dozen flat-out sprints. Keep these short – no more than 200 m (656 ft) – and fast, preferably on the flat. Their purpose is to sharpen the response of your muscles to sudden demands.

Above right: Be careful not to ride so hard in the days leading up to the race that you undo all your hard work.

Right: The rapid response work you do in the last week will help your muscles to respond to sudden changes of pace.

Left: Cross-country racing is completed on shorter circuits that demand plenty of power and acceleration.

of event. Winning times are in the three to four hour range, so top riders might not need to put in five- and six-hour sessions, and can focus on going harder on four-hour rides instead.

MULTI-STAGE RACES

Multi-stage racing demands two things of its riders: immense stamina and good recovery rates. If you are looking at training for an extreme event like the Cape Epic, which covers 920 km (570 miles) in eight days, with 16,000 m (52,480 ft)

Racing

Different types of racing demand different preparation, and the training programme on the previous pages is a very general one. There follows a look at what the different race options demand of the rider, and what refinements you might want to make to your training to be in the perfect shape.

CROSS-COUNTRY RACES

Cross-country racing is generally on shorter circuits, 6–8 km (3.7–5 miles) in length, with no long climbs but plenty of short, steep ascents, and lots of corners that slow you down and demand power to get up to speed again.

Compared to an endurance or marathon racer, the cross-country rider would need to work on pure power and acceleration, and so a shift towards shorter intervals and more repeats is the first change you

should make to the training programme. We would also not need to look at five- and six-hour rides, as the longest you could expect to be out on the course is three hours. Later on in the programme, when the expert hours continue to grow in weeks 13, 14 and 15, we would limit them to three and a half hours and raise the tempo slightly.

Cross-country racers also use their upper bodies slightly more, because they stand more on the climbs and to accelerate, so some extra work on the upper body at the gym would not be a bad idea either.

MARATHON RACES

Marathon racing is more about endurance than pure power, and the expert version of the training programme is suitable for all but riders looking at winning this type

Above: Swiss mountain biker Thomas Frischknecht is an Olympic medallist.

of altitude gained, our expert programme will fall slightly short. Extend the base period by one four-week cycle, and build up to back-to-back six-hour rides by the end of it, with a four- or five-hour ride on the Friday and a rest day on the Thursday. Through weeks 13, 14 and 15, which would now be your weeks 17, 18 and 19, double the length of all intervals, but keep the recovery period the same – this will teach your body not only to handle fatigue better, but will hopefully encourage it to not become so quickly fatigued.

24-hour races are the new craze in mountain biking, and there are two distinct categories of rider who attempt this type of event: team riders and solo riders. Team riders run a relay with three team mates, and so race a lap of a cross-country race every hour or so, for 24 hours. No special training adjustments are needed for this style of racing, just adequate rest, hydration and nutrition in between laps.

Solo riders are a different breed, and can change the course of their race with some minor adjustments to cross-country racing fitness. Whereas most cross-country racers will not need to ride for longer than three hours in their training, soloists will. They will see a slight decrease in their race speed, but will be able to hold this slower speed for much longer. Training for lack of sleep is unnecessary, in the experience of most riders, unless you plan to race like this every week.

Above: *Although downhill racing seems to require less physical fitness than other mountain biking disciplines, fitter riders definitely have the edge.*

DOWNHILL RACES

Downhill racing should, in theory, require little cardiovascular fitness, with race times of less than five minutes common. But history has shown that the fit riders who train like cross-country riders have an edge over their less sleek competitors. The big difference is that downhillers will need to spend more time in the gym developing their upper bodies than other mountain bikers, as they need more strength to wrestle the bike around, and to absorb heavy landings.

Above: *Try to get to the start line about 15 minutes in advance. You can use the time to get a good starting position, prepare yourself mentally and observe the competition. Try to keep calm and focused when the gun is fired.*

Race preparation

Race preparation is the last chance most of us have of throwing three or four months' hard work down the drain. The day of the event is not the day to discover your shoes are in your cupboard at home, in another country. It is not the day to find out that your frame is cracked, or that you didn't bring enough energy bars, or you forgot to enter. From the beginning of your racing career, no matter at what level you ride, create a system that starts with checking your equipment on your last weekend rides before the big day. Check the brakes and the gears, make sure the wheels are true, check the tyres for cuts and lubricate everything.

During the week before your race, lay out all your racing kit and tick it off against a list of which you have many copies and which does not change from week to week. Lay shoes, helmet, shirt, shorts etc. out on a table in a particular order, which also does not change from week to week. Pack it all into a race bag, putting your race numbers and documentation into a secure pocket, and all your energy sachets and food in their own pocket. The idea is to create a system that becomes second nature, but is handled in stages so that you can spot at a glance that something is missing.

The day before the race, if it is local, or the day before you leave for a non-local event, double check that you have every piece of identification, accreditation and licence you may need for the event in which you are competing. Air tickets, rental vouchers, directions to the hotel, directions from the hotel to the race venue and an idea of how long it will take to get there – all of these details need to be finalized before you leave so that when you get to your destination, the only thing you have to worry about is your race.

Above: Try not to let anyone else influence your ride – stay calm and relaxed throughout and ride your own race.

Get to the venue early enough to look at the start and finish areas. Work out your strategy for the start, where the first singletrack starts, what position you need to be in for the first corner, where bottlenecks may occur and how to get round them. If you are allowed to pre-ride the course, do so several times. If you may only walk the course – obviously possible for cross-country riders and downhillers only – do so and learn as much as you can at leisure, so that you have less to learn and think about at race pace. Check out the finish area carefully – you may be able to use your new knowledge to win a sprint to the line.

Finally, once you have changed into your race kit, go for a warm-up ride of at least 45 minutes, with a couple of sharp efforts to get the blood flowing. You can do this either with other riders or on your

own, depending on how you deal with pre-race jitters, but aim to get to the start about 15 minutes before the chutes close. This will give you time to gather yourself and your thoughts, to check out the

opposition as they arrive, and secure a good starting position, which is often critical on tight courses with early singletrack.

You have done all the hard work to get to this point. When the start gun is fired, all you can do is your best, so enjoy your ride, enjoy your race and keep calm, focused and relaxed throughout. Panic and stress have a huge negative effect, not only mentally but also physically, so try your hardest not to get caught up in the race hype and simply ride your race. Early drama is often not worth fretting about: in most races there is ample time to make up for lost time or positions. All the hard work was finished two weeks ago, all you need now is confidence in your abilities and perhaps a small amount of good fortune.

Above: All your weeks of hard work will have paid off when you finally cross that finish line. Bask in the feeling – there's nothing like it.

SAFETY

Keeping safe on mountain bikes is part common sense and part informed risk-taking, together with a healthy dose of good judgment. Prevention is far better than cure, and the following basic rules will, hopefully, guarantee you a long, safe and enjoyable mountain bike ride, and career.

Left: *Always take a map with you and know the nearest point help can be found.*

Keep hydrated

Make sure you keep drinking regularly to stave off both dehydration and heat exhaustion in warm weather.

Check the weather

Regular mountain bikers are slaves to weather reports. Keep up to date with weather forecasts so that you can dress accordingly and plan your ride.

Never ride alone

Mountain biking accidents happen in a flash and are not predictable. Never presume that you can ride alone and eliminate risk by riding an easier trail.

Plan well and know your route

Knowing where you are going and how to get back, or to the nearest dwelling, is vital. If you are riding somewhere new, either ride with locals who know the area, or make sure you have a good map. A GPS is also handy, but a hard copy of a local map could save you when the GPS battery runs out.

Tell somebody

Never leave on a ride without telling somebody where you are going and when you expect to be back. If you are riding in a group, don't presume somebody else on the ride has done this.

Never ride without a helmet

Never. Not even from your car to the trailhead – the risk just isn't worth taking.

Avoid the dark

Unless you plan a night ride and have plenty of lights, plan to end your ride at least an hour before sunset, so that if you do have problems you can still make it back to your car in daylight.

Approach animals with caution

Wild animals and horses can spook easily and react unpredictably. Approach them as cautiously as possible, without making loud noises and sudden movements.

Avoid roads

Unless you have no choice, reduce your risk of an accident by not trying to share your ride with cars, buses and trucks.

Always carry a jacket

A small windproof jacket will fit in your pocket, and may be a life saver if the weather changes. It is also useful in emergency situations, either for keeping somebody in shock warm, or for making splints or slings.

Above: *Riding in a group is a sensible option, but make sure you plan your route.*

Helmets

One of the realities of riding bikes, and not just mountain bikes, is that it is a potentially dangerous activity. Falling off a bike happens to even the best of bike handlers, and it is wise to be as prepared as possible when you set out on your ride. The most vulnerable part of your body is without doubt your head. A good helmet can be a lifesaver, no matter how slowly you think you might ride.

Helmet advocacy groups claim up to 80 per cent reduction in serious head injuries when wearing a helmet, but in reality, the numbers don't matter. Wearing a helmet should be plain common sense, and in some countries and states is mandatory.

The most basic helmets – the ones that pass the internationally respected safety standards laid out by the SNELL and ANSI organizations – are made of moulded expanded polystyrene (EPS) foam, similar to the protective packaging in which a television or a microwave is transported. The idea is that when your head strikes a hard object during a fall, the polystyrene shell compresses to absorb the impact before it reaches your skull.

Today, even the cheapest of helmets comes with a thin, plastic outer coating. This coating protects the helmet from the minor bumps and bangs it takes when it is in your sports bag or boot, but also has another, more important function.

Above: Cycling helmets are made from moulded polystyrene that compresses and absorbs the impact when your head strikes a hard object.

Above: Helmets for downhill racing are full-face in order to give greater protection. Goggles should also be worn to protect the eyes and face from branches and foliage.

Uncoated polystyrene is very soft, and can snag on the ground as you slide out of control in a fall. The plastic outer will slide, and helps stop potential neck injuries that could occur if the helmet got caught.

A number of top-end helmets now come with a nylon or Kevlar skeleton, around which the polystyrene is moulded. This skeleton is helpful in bigger crashes, where your head may strike a hard object more than once, in that it keeps the collapsed polystyrene from breaking into small pieces and leaving your head vulnerable after the first impact.

Helmets stay on your head by means of chin-straps, which should be as tight as comfortable, ensuring that the helmet does not move around as you ride, or when you fall. More up-market helmets also have a rear retention strap, either made from simple Velcro or with a ratcheting closure of some sort, which allows you to fit the helmet very securely to your head. Extra padding should be supplied with your helmet for a perfect fit. Adjust the helmet so that it does not expose your temple area – see

page 96 for a more detailed fitting guide.

Many riders refuse to wear a helmet in hot weather, claiming that it makes them hot and uncomfortable. This excuse does not hold water, as modern helmets are better ventilated than ever before, and some of the top models will actually keep your head cooler than wearing no helmet. When looking at a helmet's ventilation, don't just look at the number of ventilation holes, look at how they channel the air over your head. On cheaper helmets, the top holes will seem to point straight to your head when looked at from above. All that will happen here is

that most of the air will pass over the top of your head, providing little benefit. A more expensive moulding setup will allow the air to flow more evenly over and around your head.

Some cross-country helmets come with a fine mesh blocking the forward-facing air vents. This is to keep bugs and beetles out – there is little more distressing on a bike than trying to rapidly decelerate and remove your helmet without angering the stinging insect that is now buzzing in your hair.

The only discipline that requires a special helmet is downhilling. Most downhillers wear full-face motorcycle-type helmets, for the added protection needed on the dangerous courses they ride. This helmet is also made from lightweight polystyrene, and comes without a visor.

Above: The ventilation holes should channel the air over your scalp and help to cool your head. A quick-release chin strap makes it easy to take on and off.

Essential kit

Basic safety gear can turn a potentially life-threatening situation out on the trail into just another adventure story. Safety on shorter rides is simpler to equip for, and taking a mobile phone, the basic tools and spares laid out on pages 88–89 and remembering to tell somebody responsible exactly where you are going and when you expect to be back should suffice.

If you are doing longer rides, or rides in areas that are remote, you will need to be better prepared and more fully equipped. For longer rides make sure that there is at least one of each of the following in your group. Preferably, each person should have all these items just in case anyone in the group finds themselves isolated, for whatever reason.

1 Duct tape

Almost anything can be fixed, rigged, repaired and made to work again with this miracle tape.

2 GPS (not shown)

If your budget extends to one of these, get one. It will not only allow you to pin-point where you are to a metre or so, helping rescuers to find you, but most models let you retrace your steps should you get lost.

3 Space blanket

Perfect for warming riders in shock, or for bedding down for an unplanned night under the stars.

4 Lightweight windbreaker

Perfect for changes in weather, keeping crash victims warm when in shock, or for strapping wounds and making a sling should you need to strap a shoulder or collarbone injury.

5 Tubes

Always carry at least two tubes.

6 First-aid kit

Including plasters, bandages, scissors, sutures, needles, antiseptic, painkillers and water-purifying tablets.

7 Pump

Forgetting your pump just once will teach you how essential this item is.

8 Puncture kit

Never leave home without one – you never know when one will strike.

9 Emergency rations

Always take some extra energy bars in case you run out of fuel on a ride that takes longer than expected.

10 Compass

In case your GPS loses power.

11 Chain tool

A lightweight chain tool will make the difference between riding and walking home.

12 Map

A map of the area, even if you know it well, may help you guide emergency personnel to your location.

13 Emergency lights

A pair of small LED lights will cost little in the way of weight or space but, if you manage to overdo things and stay out after dark, will give enough light to make it back to the car or make repairs. If you need to ride on public roads to get home after dark, flashing lights will make you more visible to other road users.

14 Multi-tool

Light and compact, with 2.5, 4, 5 and 6 mm Allen keys and flat- and star/cross-head screwdrivers.

15 Whistle

Useful for calling for help or calling your riding partners when you have a problem.

16 Identification

Always carry identification with telephone numbers of people other than those you are riding with and your medical details. In a waterproof plastic bag, your ID will double up as a gaiter for a cut tyre.

17 Mobile or satellite phone

Being able to call for help and tell rescuers where you are, what is wrong and what you need from them is vital. Mobile phones are limited in range, but a satellite phone will work virtually anywhere.

19 Tyre levers

Vital when it is cold and wet, or when your hands are sweaty and slippery.

18 Money

Always take some cash in case you need to make phone calls or buy food to top up your energy levels.

Navigation and planning

The first step to safe and successful mountain bike expeditions is careful planning and a basic knowledge of navigation. In the next few pages we will attempt to go through the basics of both, but navigation is worth studying in more detail if you are planning to do some ambitious exploring. There are a number of very good books on the subject, which your local bookseller should be able to recommend to you.

Planning a safe trip will involve three elements: choosing a route, choosing your riding partners and choosing good weather. Plan your route carefully, using a map and speaking to riders who may have done a similar route and getting their advice. Try to find a 1:50,000

scale map as it will show detail as fine as footpaths. Looking at contours and probable trail conditions, you should be able to estimate the length of time it will take to cover your chosen route. Factor in time for punctures and possible crashes, as well as for getting lost in places. Remember to inform somebody who will not

be going with you of your plans and when you expect to return.

If you are making an expedition deep into the wilderness, your choice of riding partners will be an important factor in its success. Look for equal or similarly matched fitness levels, as any differences will be exaggerated after a few hours riding, and could degenerate into frustration and conflict if the group has to keep waiting for a slower rider. It is also a good idea, if you are riding far from your normal mountain biking areas, to get hold of local mountain bikers and see if there are some that would be willing to show you the way. Not only will it reduce your chances of getting lost, but they might show you

Right: Mountain biking in the wilderness can be a dangerous activity without proper planning and organization.

better riding than you had planned on your map.

The final factor, and most difficult to prepare for or predict, is the weather. The internet is a wonderful resource for local weather forecasts, and you should also be able to find out what the typical weather patterns for that area at that time of year are likely to be. However, no weather forecast is a cast-iron guarantee, so pack some extra warm and cold weather gear. You can always leave it in the car at the start of the ride, but if you haven't brought it and the weather surprises you, you have no choice in the matter.

Planning for multi-day tours is more difficult, and more important. You will need to plan virtually every step of your journey. You will need to decide if you are going to camp – which will mean carrying tents, cooking equipment and food, reducing your daily mileage – or take what is known as the 'credit card tour'.

Credit card touring involves staying in hotels or bed and breakfasts, and eating in restaurants. The advantages are obvious: warm beds, warm showers and being waited on will make for a relaxing, enjoyable tour. But it is an expensive way of travelling, and some would say it is removed from real mountain bike touring: you will certainly miss out on some of the sights, sounds and smells of the wilderness.

Either way, decent maps and detailed planning of every day's route will make your adventure a pleasing, successful one.

Below: Prepare for any eventuality with the weather and always take plenty of spare warm and cold weather gear. A waterproof jacket is a must.

Above: Learning how to read a map and use a compass are important skills if you want to continue mountain biking in safety.

Topographical maps are available from the mapping departments of most local governments, and the best resolution for mountain bike expeditions is a 1:50,000 scale. This will give you details such as footpaths, dwellings and farm buildings. The contours are close enough together to accurately predict the ups and downs of the trail, but will be big enough to cover all but the longest rides on one map. One centimetre on the map relates to 500 metres out on the trail.

Protecting the map from the elements is important, so buy a waterproof pouch with a clear cover so that you can read the map through it without getting it drenched.

The next step is finding a good compass. It needs to be easy to read, robust, large enough to be useful but small enough to stow easily, and the needle should be in a liquid container, not an air one, so that it settles more quickly. A magnifying glass with a ruler down one edge is also useful.

The most important thing to remember when using a compass is to keep it away from any ferrous metal. This includes bikes, watches, fences – anything that is made of or contains steel can affect the reading you get. There is

Basic navigation

We spend a fair portion of our lives navigating without even realizing it. We do this by remembering landmarks and where they fit in with other landmarks on maps we carry in our minds. Familiarity with our surroundings makes this simple, and we rarely get lost in our hometown, but as soon as we move into new surroundings it becomes more difficult. We have to start all over again, mentally building a new map of a new area.

Above: Topographical maps for mountain biking should be on a scale of 1:50,000 and should include details such as trails, paths and buildings.

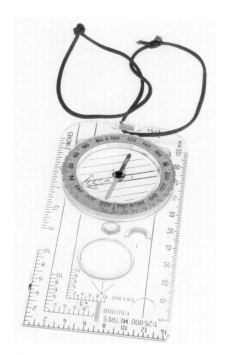

Above: Remember to keep your compass away from any ferrous metal, or the reading you get may not be accurate.

beacons, buildings or forks in the road.

Learn how information provided on a map relates to the real world. Most hills or mountains have distinct shapes, and an experienced map-reader will know, by looking at the contours, what they should look like. The closer together contours are on the map, the steeper the terrain. Learn what sort of spacing tests your limits, and if a road looks too long and steep, look for a way around it.

Estimating distance on a map is a matter of tracing your route out in a 2B pencil – dark enough to see and easily erasable – and following it, estimating a centimetre at a time. Add up the number of centimetres, divide by two for a 1:50,000 map, and you get a rough idea of how far in kilometres you are going to be riding. The more accurate way is to buy a map-measuring wheel – a device that has a small wheel at one end and a dial or digital read-out that clocks up distance as you roll it along your intended route. These devices, however, are likely to give an approximate shorter distance, as they can't take into account the natural weaving course a rider follows on a trail to find a line and avoid obstacles. To get an idea of the scale of allowance (e.g. plus two per cent), measure a known route first so that you have something to apply to future calculations.

a difference between true north, which is what maps work with, and the magnetic north your compass will show. The difference, in degrees, will be printed in the key to the map, so remember to take this into account when navigating. It differs from country to country, but shouldn't be more than a couple of degrees.

The best way to work with a map and a compass together is to hold them in one hand, with the grid lines on the map and the compass needle aligned. Work out where you are, work out where you need to be going on the map and start looking for cross-references between the map and your surroundings, like mountains, trig

Above: A map wheel will give you a more accurate estimation of distance, but your course will probably weave about more than you allow for.

Responding to emergency

One of the realities of mountain biking is that it is a potentially dangerous sport. Fortunately, few of us will ever find ourselves in a life-threatening situation out on the bike, but it does no harm to have a basic idea of how to cope with possible eventualities.

Hypothermia is a real risk for mountain bikers. Changes in weather can be sudden. It is also all too easy to lose track of time and distance and stay out on the bike longer than expected. Exhaustion will accelerate hypothermia, as will dehydration, so make sure you drink lots of fluid, especially in cold weather. Post-crash shock can also bring on hypothermia in lower temperatures.

The initial symptoms of hypothermia are cold and numb extremities, with intermittent shivering. If the shivering becomes more violent and less controllable, and you begin to feel lethargic, light-headed and struggle to focus, start treating these symptoms as hypothermia.

Get rid of any wet clothing and replace with warm, dry kit. The aim is to warm the body up slowly, as a rapid increase in temperature can put strain on your heart. A space blanket is perfect for this, and in extreme cases you can use another person's body-heat wrapped in the same space blanket to accelerate the process. Take in as much fluid as

Above: *Mountain biking can be potentially dangerous, so familiarizing yourself with basic first aid is a very sensible idea.*

possible, as the chances are that dehydration is a factor too. Get medical help as quickly as you can.

Heat exposure and heatstroke are as dangerous as hypothermia, but are relatively simple to avoid and manage. The first thing to do is to drink lots of fluid – at least a litre per hour – and ride out of the heat of the midday sun where possible. Drinking a formula that

includes some isotonic ingredients can help to replenish some of the minerals you sweat out in the heat. Sunblock will help to keep you cool by preventing sunburn, so make sure you reapply it regularly.

The symptoms of heatstroke are obvious, but manifest very quickly. The main signs are a high temperature, a slightly confused state, and dry, flushed skin as the

Above: Cuts and grazes from falls are relatively easy to deal with, provided you have a basic first aid kit with you.

need to perform Cardio Pulmonary Resuscitation (CPR). Tilt the head back slightly, pinch the nostrils shut, put your mouth over the victim's and breathe out strongly, forcing air into their lungs. The victim's chest should rise and fall as if they are breathing when you do this properly. Repeat roughly 12 times per minute until the victim is breathing unaided.

Whilst you are helping with breathing, check for a pulse using the artery in the neck. No pulse means alternating the breathing with heart massage, where you stimulate the heart into beating by depressing the victim's ribcage. These techniques are best learned and practised at a recognised first-aid school, and hopefully you will never need them. But they may just save a life.

body's sweat mechanisms fail to keep the skin moist. This is a potentially lethal condition, so once you think there is a danger of a rider getting heatstroke, act quickly. Get the victim into shade if possible and cover them with wet clothing and towels while fanning them, to get a cool air moving over them. A cold bath or shower, if available, will accelerate recovery, as will rehydrating. Qualified medical help should be summoned if the victim's condition doesn't start to improve.

ACCIDENT RESPONSE

Accidents happen to the best of riders. The first thing to do is take stock of injuries. The basic tenets of first aid are the ABCs: airway, breathing and circulation.

Whether conscious or unconscious, do not move the crash victim, or roll them over, until you have ascertained whether there are spinal injuries. Do not remove clothing or helmets unless they are restricting breathing. The first job is to ensure the airways are not blocked, so check that there is nothing blocking the throat – vomit, false teeth and any food that may have been in the mouth at the time of falling. If the victim's tongue has rolled back into their throat, pull it forward until the airway is clear.

Breathing is the next priority, and if they are not breathing, you will

Above: Heatstroke is common in warmer climes. Symptoms include flushed skin, a high temperature and confusion.

Left: *If you crash out in a race, there will be plenty of medical personnel on hand to treat your injuries and make sure you have not done any serious damage.*

Below: *Crashing on a trail may just bruise your ego more than anything else. Protective clothing will shield you from most cuts and grazes.*

Once the ABCs have been checked, you'll need to check for cuts, gashes and broken bones. The most common broken bone in cycling is the collarbone, normally caused when you put an arm out to stop a fall. In the event of a broken collarbone, you will need to get the victim off the mountain as fast and as safely as possible, with the injured arm strapped for maximum comfort. Put the forearm on the injured side across the chest and use a jacket or bandages to hold the arm in place. Understandably, this will be a painful process, but once it is strapped up, the victim will be as comfortable as can be expected.

Separated shoulders are also a regular mountain bike injury, and there is a temptation to treat them with less urgency than a broken collarbone. The danger with this is that you can do even more damage by trying to ride off the mountain to find help. Rather treat it in the same way – strap the arm to the body as you would for a collarbone – and walk the victim to a point where emergency services or some other form of transport

Above: *If a rider seems confused and disorientated after a fall, they may be concussed. Get them to a hospital as soon as possible.*

you have managed to arrange can get them to specialized help as soon as possible.

Head injuries are also a reality, and if the victim is unconscious and you have gone through the ABCs without any sign of rousing, get help as soon as possible. When you make contact with emergency services, it is important that you tell them every detail you can so that they can come as prepared as possible. If the victim remains unconscious, stay with them and keep an eye on their breathing and pulse.

Conscious victims of head injuries may be disorientated and delirious. Concussion is very serious, and you need to get them to an emergency room as quickly as possible. Keep the victim moving at all times, or make sure if they are injured too badly to move, that they stay awake. Keep them talking, get them to describe their surroundings, talk about last weekend's ride, anything to keep the brain awake and active.

For the treatment of cuts and gashes, you should have a basic first aid kit with you, and mostly you will not need more than a bit of disinfectant to clean the wound. Once you have cleaned it, cover it with plasters to keep grit out. If you are out in the middle of nowhere and have a cut that may require stitches, try taping it closed with plasters and bandages. Learning to suture out on the trail is difficult and will almost guarantee an infection – it is definitely best left to medically qualified personnel.

Getting off the mountain after an accident is a long and tiresome process, both for the victim and the rescuer. If you have shoulder or arm injuries, do not be tempted to try to ride down. Riding with one hand is asking for a second crash. It's better to walk and push the bike, keeping a slow but steady pace, drinking regularly and keeping yourself and your rescuers in as good spirits as possible.

NUTRITION

Success in mountain biking, however you measure it, is dependent on two things: a mechanically sound machine and a well-maintained motor. That motor is you, and a healthy, balanced diet can make the difference between a good race and a win, or a fun day out and a depressing, long ride home.

Critical to your success and enjoyment on the bike is a combination of nutrition, hydration and sensible supplementation. Each of these individual elements is important, but the combination, in the right balance, will transform your riding, allowing you to train harder, race harder and finish rides feeling strong. Most riders consider nutrition in a race situation, or when they are spending all day exploring new trails. This is the easy part, where a few energy bars and a pocketful of energy sachets will give your body the fuel it needs to complete the job in hand. But the longer-term view is more difficult. A balanced day-to-day diet is the key to getting to the starting line fresh and ready to use your body to its fullest potential.

A good diet will give you enough energy to complete your training and recover in time for your next session. It should supply roughly the correct ratio of protein, carbohydrate and unsaturated fat, avoiding the saturated fat that leads to cholesterol build-up and other potentially dangerous side effects.

Your body burns energy whether you are exercising or not. The majority of this energy is taken from your fat reserves, which can store in excess of 100,000 calories in the average male. This average male will use in the region of 2,000 calories just to keep the mind and body functioning, and the average female 1,500 calories, before any

Above: Fruit doesn't have to be boring: bananas, kiwi and strawberries make a delicious snack.

consideration is given to exercising.

At full tilt, an athlete can burn about 1,000 calories in an hour, but the rest of us are more likely to burn 500–600 calories an hour on a hard ride, and 200–300 calories on an easy ride. So, if you are training a moderate two hours a day, you would need to increase your calorie intake by at least 500 calories.

The timing of the ingestion of these calories is also important. Your body is in full recovery mode in the hour after you have exercised, so it is important to take in as much as you can in that time period. Sports scientists have calculated an ideal of 70 grams of carbohydrate and a litre of liquid as being about as much as the body can handle in this time frame, with a small amount of protein. This will help replenish the glycogen stores in your muscles at a time when they

are at their most receptive.

Supplementation is one of the most overlooked areas in nutrition. At a basic level, a good multi-vitamin taken daily will redress any minor imbalances in a person's diet, but, for the dedicated racer, protein shakes and targeted supplementation in areas of their diet that are lacking are a hugely important part of training.

Balance is the key to a dietary plan that works, and that you can stick to. Most of us can improve our eating habits easily. For some, what is needed is a complete overhaul. Make changes gradually. If you are eating four chocolate bars a day and you need to cut them out, don't stop overnight; change gradually and it will be easier to sustain your new eating habits long enough for them to become your new routine.

Above: A healthy diet with plenty of fruit and vegetables will improve your fitness and your performance on the bike.

Above: Low GI carbohydrates include rye bread, sweet potatoes, spaghetti, pearl barley, macaroni, porridge oats and bran.

Food building blocks

There are three food groups that keep our bodies running efficiently. The first is the athlete's favourite – carbohydrates. These are the basic energy blocks that the body uses to convert glucose to glycogen, which gets stored in the liver and the muscles. This is the body's most readily available source of instant energy. Once these reserves are used up, the body digs into fat reserves, but can only process these reserves slowly, so keeping your carbohydrate levels up is vital. Roughly 60 per cent of your daily intake should come in the form of carbohydrates – about 5 grams per kilogram of body weight.

Not all carbohydrates are created equal. They are measured on a scale called the glycaemic index, which gives you an idea of how quickly or slowly they are digested, and how quickly your body will be able to use them as energy. Pasta and potatoes are examples of low GI foods, which should be taken regularly during the day, and in the build-up to a big ride, while high GI foods include energy gels and the like – perfect for ingesting whilst on the bike, for instant energy. GI can also be affected by cooking and preparation methods – baked, mashed and fried potatoes, for instance, all have vastly differing indices – and there are far too many variables to cover in this book.

Protein is the building block for your muscles. Training is a process – at a biokinetic level – that creates tiny tears in your muscle fibres, which are repaired and made stronger than they were before your exercise session. The amino acids in protein are vital to this process, and in recent years protein has taken an ever-increasingly important place in the athlete's diet. The body does not have the capacity to store protein, so it is important to maintain a daily ingestion rate of about 1.5 grams of protein per kilogram of body weight.

The best sources of protein are red meat, fish and nuts. Fat and protein are often found side-by-side in the same foods, and fish is arguably the healthiest option, followed by lean red meat – with fat

Above: A healthy balance of carbohydrates, protein and fat will keep mountain bikers in peak condition.

Right: Polyunsaturated fats are found in avacados, almonds, walnuts and cashews. They help your body absorb vitamins.
Below: Vegetarians need high protein foods such as broccoli, sweetcorn, tomatoes, peas, mushrooms and beans.

trimmed and grilled rather than fried – and finally nuts. There are a number of high-protein vegetables, but they do not necessarily contain the specific amino acids that your body requires. Vegetarians can train effectively without eating meat, but will need to eat a variety of vegetables to do so.

Fats are widely regarded as anathema to healthy eating, but they are actually critical in proper nutrition. They are an essential long-term energy source, called upon when the body is running out of glycogen, and are important, through their cholesterol and phospholipids content, in the rebuilding of muscle fibres. The problem with fats is that, unlike protein, which the body converts to energy and flushes the rest, excess fat is retained in the body.

The trick to getting enough fat in your diet – roughly 1 gram per kilogram of bodyweight a day – without it going on your waist or hips, is eating the right type of fat. Avoid saturated fats as far as you can – things like sausages, crisps and fried breakfasts – and concentrate on monounsaturated and polyunsaturated fats found in foods such as olive oil,

walnuts, almonds, cashews and avocados. These unsaturated fats also help your body to absorb vitamins. There are two rules of thumb that will help in the quest to avoid bad fats. First, look at the food label. Anything containing fewer than 5 grams of

fat per 100 grams can be regarded as low fat. If the food does not have a label, the second way is to avoid fats that are solids at room temperature. These 'rules' will not guarantee food to be saturate-free, but you won't be far wrong and your diet will be healthier.

Supplements

Supplementation is a vital element in an athlete's effective nutritional program. Vitamins and minerals are the unseen boosters that keep an athlete on top form, fuelling chemical and biological processes throughout the body. Deficiencies in any particular area can see the body robbing other areas to make up the shortfall, setting up a chain of deficiencies that can lead to reduced performance.

Vitamins help the body with basic metabolism, but are almost more important in fighting free-radicals, the by-products of metabolism that can cause illness. Exercise causes the loss of vitamins through sweating, so for athletes it is important to keep vitamin levels topped up. This is possible through eating fresh fruit and vegetables, but with today's hectic lifestyle, supplementation is a secure way of ensuring optimal vitamin levels.

The most common vitamins you will need to keep an eye on are C, B and E, and a group called the flavanoids. Vitamin C combats illness and can help reduce bad and increase good cholesterol in your body. Orange juice is the most common source, and a slight overdosing of vitamin C can be tolerated by the body.

Vitamin B has a number of varieties, all of which contribute to more efficient metabolism. Vitamin E helps with recovery and cell regrowth, and boosts your immune system. Shellfish is a good source,

Left: Taking supplementary vitamins can help to boost your immune system and make up for any deficiencies in your diet.

and also contains the antioxidants selenium and zinc, which further aid recovery. Other vitamin E sources are nuts, spinach and pulses.

Flavanoids are powerful antioxidants, and will help with recovery and general health. They naturally occur in tangerines, guavas and tomatoes.

Mineral replenishment is also critical, as minerals are critical to the day-to-day running of the body. Individually, all of these substances have a role, but collectively, you can keep them topped up with a good multi-vitamin pill, taken daily.

Sodium is possibly the most important, as it helps control the absorption of fluids into the body. Look for a sports drink that contains sodium, and use it both in training and racing.

Iron is the most commonly deficient mineral in athletes, and is

key to the amount of oxygen the red blood cells can carry to the muscles, where it is needed. Vegetarians, especially, need to supplement iron levels as few vegetables can provide enough on a daily basis. Iron deficiency is easily recognizable through a pale complexion and reduced energy levels.

Omega-3 fatty acids are needed to help boost your immune system, and are found in fish such as tuna and salmon. They are good for your brain too, so keep yourself tactically on top with some tuna!

Potassium will help you to avoid sodium loss in the body, and is found in bananas. It also helps with your hydration systems, and magnesium helps with muscle contraction. Combined, these two substances are linked, by many, to cramp prevention, and even if there is little scientific evidence either way, maintaining a healthy balance through your sports drink is a good idea.

Choosing a multi-vitamin supplement pill is not easy, as there are many on the market. Most sports nutritionists recommend that you look for something that offers 100 per cent of the recommended daily allowance of each, and no more. Some advocate overdosing on certain minerals and vitamins, but rather do that through natural

Above: *Flavanoids are powerful antioxidants and are found in pears, apricots, apples and berries.*

sources, not artificially, as there is no scientific proof that it has any effect.

Creatine has been used in many sports to enhance performance. To date, no long-term side effects of creatine supplementation have been found, but the substance is relatively new, so keep up to date if you do use it. It is found naturally in red meat and accelerates the body's ATP replenishment, aiding recovery. It allows athletes to train harder and build more lean muscle. Some athletes swear by it, others see no difference; all users have reported the need for increased hydration levels when using it.

Caffeine is a daily part of modern life, and not just for athletes. It is a natural stimulant and can form an important part of a training regime. Moderate amounts of caffeine stimulate the mitochondria – the energy-producing parts of your cells – to work more efficiently, so energy gets released more quickly. Current thinking is that excess caffeine is expelled by the body – hence the need to urinate after a few cups of coffee – and that there are no long-term negative effects on the body, so a cup before you ride will give you the get-up-and-go to ride effectively.

Above: *As a natural stimulant, caffeine can form part of your training regime.*

A balanced diet

The biggest challenge most amateur athletes face when it comes to nutrition is keeping control of a balanced diet during a hectic working day. This takes almost as much discipline as trying to fit in the training and recovery you need to achieve your goals. The key to successfully staying on the right track with your diet is to eat small amounts of food, often. This will help you manage your blood sugar levels through the day – no post-lunch slump – and will leave you with more than enough energy to train after work. The best bet is to split your day into five separate sections, plus one extra for every training session you do.

The first meal of the day is breakfast. If you train in the mornings, you might need a snack to get your body up and running before you leave – a banana or a slice of toast with jam or honey. Breakfast is the meal that will set the tone for the rest of the day, and something like three wholewheat biscuits with 250 ml (9 fl oz) skimmed milk and two slices of wholemeal bread is a good start to the day. Use an olive-oil based spread, and a small amount of jam or honey to flavour the toast. This will give you about 95 g (3¼ oz) carbohydrate, 7 g (⅛ oz) fat and 10 g (¼ oz) protein

Next is the mid-morning snack, which you are advised to prepare at home. A bread roll with some cottage cheese – avoid other cheeses as they are usually high in saturated fat – and 200 ml (7 fl oz) of orange juice will give you a 65 g (3 oz) carbohydrate/14 g (½ oz) fat/ 10 g (¼ oz) protein boost to tide you over until lunch.

Lunch is a dangerous time, as the canteen may well not cater to the nutritional needs of an athlete. Your goal should be something like a large baked potato with a low fat topping devoid of cheese, bacon, or anything else fatty. A small amount of cream cheese or cottage cheese will be fine. Supplement this with a yoghurt and a 500 ml (8 fl oz) sports drink, and you will have another 120 g (4¼ oz) carbohydrate and 15–20 g (½–¾ oz) protein in the bank. An alternative to this could be a green salad, with balsamic vinegar instead of salad dressing, and some sliced bread with a low-fat topping.

Your mid-afternoon snack is a reward meal, so grab a 30 g (1 oz) chocolate bar or a banana, and a glass of skimmed milk or a small yoghurt. Add 40 g (1½ oz) carbohydrate/10 g (¼ oz) fat/5 g (⅛ oz) protein to the day's total.

Dinner is the recovery meal for the day, the one that sets you up for a good sleep, and a refreshed start to the following day. A medium portion of rice, 150 g (5½ oz) lean meat or fish, and a green salad or some steamed vegetables will set you up well, and will contribute 50 g (2¼ oz) carbohydrates, 40 g (1½ oz) protein and 20 g (¾ oz) fat to your day. A dessert of 100 g (4 oz) sorbet will give you another 25g (1 oz)

Left: A good breakfast of wheat cereal, toast and jam will set you up for a day of hard training.

carbohydrates, leaving you with a total for the day of roughly 400 g (14 oz) of carbohydrates, 85 g (3 oz) of protein and 50 g (2 oz) of unsaturated fat. You will have to add to this whatever recovery nutrition you take after your training, whether it is in the form of a shake or solid food, but for a basic day of quality, balanced nutrition, this should be adequate. If you find yourself hungry in between these regular eating times, eat an apple or a pear – any light fruit that will just boost the blood sugar for a short while.

Deliberately left out of this plan, because it is vitally important in its own right, is water. Try to drink 300 ml (10 fl oz) of water every hour through the day to avoid dehydration and aid digestion and energy absorption.

Alcohol intake should be kept to a minimum, as it is not easily digested and the body will call on other carbohydrate sources first. If the body is happy with the amount of glycogen in its various storage facilities, the alcohol will be metabolized to fat, for storage for a later date. Don't avoid alcohol totally, though, as a glass of red wine will give you a good boost of antioxidants.

Top: *A mid-morning snack of cottage cheese, a wholemeal roll and a glass of orange juice will fill you up until lunch.*
Right: *Lunch could be a green salad with balsamic vinegar and wholemeal bread.*

Above: Don't forget to pay attention to your nutrition in the lead-up to a big race. What you eat has a huge effect on the way you perform.

Preparing to race

Preparing your nutritional regime for an important event is critical, and it is amazing how many athletes train for months, spend a fortune on the best equipment and then are too nervous to eat dinner the night before, or breakfast the day of the event. A loss of appetite before a big event is natural, as your nervous system goes into hyperdrive. A controlled eating plan the week before the event, and on the morning, will help keep the butterflies in your stomach flying in formation.

For races lasting less than an hour and a half, there is not much point in adjusting your daily routine, as your body will have stored enough glycogen, in normal circumstances, to get you through an event this short. It is when you want to race longer than that you will need to change your routine.

Carb-loading is a technique that has been used, in different guises and to different extremes, for many years to first deprive the body of its usual daily amount of carbohydrates, and then cram as many in as possible in the days before the event. Originally, it was a brutal regime of three days of full training, taking in absolutely no carbohydrate, followed by three days of light training and as much pasta and bread as you could eat. The principle is to deprive the body of carbohydrates, and eventually its defence mechanisms will start aggressively storing more glycogen than usual, just in case this 'famine' is a long-term problem. Once it has been duped in this way, exploit this defence mechanism and overload with carbohydrates.

The theory of this nutritional ploy was correct, but the execution was appalling, as the depletion phase often left athletes overtired for the race, and any excess carbohydrates that could not be turned to glycogen were turned to fatty deposits in the loading phase. Modern thinking is to stick to a similar programme, but in the six- to four-day period before the event, reduce carbohydrate intake to about 50 per cent instead of the usual 60, while halving the amount of training done each day. The first day of this reduced depletion phase should contain at least one half-hour high intensity session, to fine-tune the body's responses to your tapering phase.

Three days before the event, increase the carbohydrate portion of your diet to roughly 70 per cent, splitting the remaining 30 per cent evenly between proteins and fats. Training should now reduce to nothing two days before the event, but take a short leg-loosener the day before with one or two bursts of race-pace riding to prime the muscles and make sure the carbohydrates are being stored efficiently. Your body can only absorb, at its most efficient, about 100 g (4 oz) of carbohydrate an hour, so don't waste money on expensive loading drinks – your normal diet with one or two extra sports drinks and a bigger portion of rice with your evening meal will do the trick.

The final meal before you race is critical, as it will set you up for the period after an hour and a half of racing. Choose low-glycaemic index foods that will be absorbed slowly and give you a slower energy release, almost like a long-term investment at the bank. They will give you lower energy levels, but for much longer. It is important to have a balanced meal, fairly similar to your normal diet, so as not to upset your stomach and to ensure you keep a healthy balance of vitamins and minerals. A huge plate of plain pasta is not ideal; less pasta with some vegetables and strips of fish or lean beef will be better.

Breakfast on the morning of the ride is more to kick-start the engine than to fill the tank – that should have been done the week and day before. A couple of slices of toast with low-fat spread and jam will normally do the trick, with a 500 ml (18 fl oz) energy drink to maximize your hydration and a banana. Eating more than this and trying to race your heart out a few hours later could cause stomach upsets or

cramps as the glycogen needed for digestion will be called away and sent to your muscles. If you have an afternoon race, then a big breakfast is fine, just make sure you have a good three to four hours to let it all digest, and then have some toast and jam an hour before you start.

Top: *An ideal pre-race meal is pasta with vegetables and fish – plain enough not to upset your stomach.*
Above: *Six to four days before your race, reduce your carbohydrate intake whilst continuing your training rides.*

179

Above: Bananas and fruitcake are both ideal energy replacement snacks. Make sure you eat small amounts regularly to avoid your energy levels dropping.

Energy levels

If you are going to be riding for longer than an hour and a half, you will need to carry some form of energy replacement with you. This can take the form of energy syrup sachets, energy bars, bananas or fruitcake, depending on how far and hard you are riding.

As with hydration, the trick is to eat small amounts as regularly as you can, and to eat before you feel hungry. One of the most frightening experiences you will ever have on a bike – and we all do it once – is what is known as bonking. This is the pause between your body running out of short-term glycogen supplies and its slow switchover to burning fat. Your body shuts down all the energy systems, pedalling becomes a struggle and you feel light-headed and weak. There really is no way to describe it fully, but it is well worth never experiencing.

Keeping your glycogen levels up is relatively simple, but takes discipline. Start by popping an energy sachet into your mouth just before the start, no matter how long your race is going to last. For shorter events – under an hour and a half – this should suffice, but anything longer than that and you will need to keep replenishing every 45 minutes to an hour, with either more gel sachets, energy bars or bananas. Do not wait until you feel you are running out of energy to start replenishing – it will be too late. The target is to get 50–70 g (2¼–3¼ oz) of carbohydrate into your system every hour, washed down with water to help digestion.

Your choice of fuel will be personal, but is often dictated by the type of event and the pace you will be riding at. Energy bars are great for energy delivery and replacing minerals, but at full race pace, you might find it hard to chew, breathe and swallow at the same time. For cross-country racing and top-end marathon races, gel sachets are the ideal answer – you bite a corner off and squeeze the contents into your mouth, swallow, and you have the required amount of carbohydrate quickly and cleanly administered.

The downside of these gel products is that they generally have a very high glycaemic index and, while they digest quickly and are absorbed faster than any other form, the energy gets burned very quickly. For longer rides, you will need to balance regular ingestion of these sachets with an occasional banana or energy bar, which both contain lower glycaemic index carbohydrates that will release more slowly and help you avoid sugar spikes, and the ensuing sugar lows. Long races on just gel sachets require absolute dedication to eating them every 45 minutes; miss a feed and it is extremely hard to

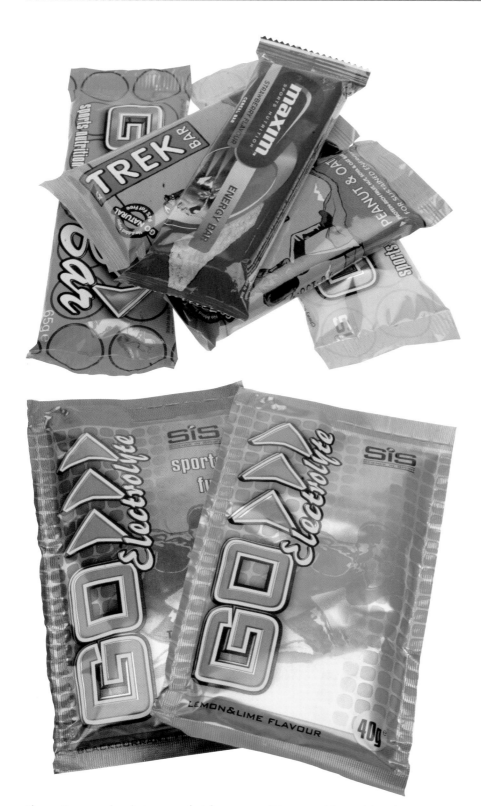

get your sugar levels up again.

Longer races, stage races and all-day adventures allow you to have some variety. After a few hours, energy bars and gel sachets can become tedious. Balance them with a banana or two, and possibly even a ham sandwich or some fruit cake. Be sure to take something savoury, not for the energy it contains but just to break the monotony of sweet things passing your lips. The salty taste will make you feel much better.

What you drink is also important, and it is best, on longer rides, to have a proper sports drink mixture in your bottle. Be careful with ready-mixed versions, as the concentration may be too strong when you have been racing for a few hours, and you may develop stomach troubles.

Which brings us to possibly the most important advice you will ever hear regarding on-the-bike nutrition: never, ever try something new in a race or an important event. There is always the chance it will not agree with you, so test it out in training several weeks before your big event. And on the day, make the concentration a tiny bit weaker. Racing on an upset stomach is not just unpleasant, it is dangerous, as it greatly accelerates the process of dehydration.

Above: Energy gel sachets are perfect for race conditions, providing quick carbs when you need them most.

Hydration

Staying hydrated is the biggest challenge to most endurance athletes and, as a mountain biker, you will probably be better equipped than most: you get to carry up to 3 litres (5 pints) of liquid in a hydration pack. Planning your hydration strategy involves two major considerations: you need to make sure you have enough to drink for the full duration of the event – plus some to spare in case of emergencies – and you need to decide what you are going to drink.

The aim is to drink a litre (1¾ pts) of liquid every hour of the event. Start with half a litre (18 fl oz) of energy drink half an hour before you start – allowing enough time to visit the toilet – and then concentrate on taking small sips as often as you can throughout the event. If you are racing, you can try to gauge how long you are going to be out there, and carry just enough water, but only do this if you are sure there are watering stations on the route should a mechanical problem or a fall keep you out longer than expected.

Marathon events will tend to have watering points spread over the second half of the course, but do not rely on making it to any one of them having just finished your water. Rather stop and refill your hydration pack at a water point before you run out. The penalty for dehydration is a loss of strength, possible cramping and, if you let it go too far, light-headedness and an

Above: Hydration is key when racing. You should aim to drink a litre (1¾ pints) of liquid for every hour you compete.

impairment to concentration. You will not be able to reverse these symptoms quickly or easily once they have set in, and certainly not in enough time to carry on riding in any decent capacity, so rather err on the side of caution and carry a little too much liquid.

The same goes for touring and exploring. If you find a stream or a farmhouse, and your water supply is half-depleted, fill up there and then. Even if the map shows a dwelling or a stream an hour away, you might find it deserted or dried up when you get there.

The latest research into hydration has revealed a disturbing condition called over-hydration (hyponatraemia), which can lead to water intoxication: basically, too much water can be deadly. This was first observed and researched in IronMan athletes, where a number of participants at the top end of the field finished well, but marginally dehydrated, whereas athletes further back finished in a poor state, often collapsing at the finish. This was not just because they had been competing for longer, but because they had ritually been forcing water into their bodies, fearful of dehydration.

The key to avoiding this condition, which is essentially a reaction to diluted sodium levels in the body, is to make sure you don't force a drink down if it doesn't feel right to, and make sure you use an energy drink with a reasonable concentration of sodium and other minerals. Plain water is fine for races that will only last an hour or so, but if you are going to be riding longer than that, an energy/mineral replenishment drink is vital. Using a carbohydrate replacement drink makes sense anyway, as it is an easy way to keep your energy levels topped up.

Away from the racing scene for a moment, it can sometimes be difficult to find man-made watering holes when you are exploring new trails and roads. You will sometimes

Above: Energy gels are better than plain water if you are competing in longer races.

Above: Don't force liquid down if it doesn't feel right to – hyponatraemia could be the potentially fatal result.

be required to refill hydration packs from streams or rivers. The first rule of thumb for deciding whether this water is safe or not is to look on a map, or just look at your surroundings and gauge whether there is a dwelling or a village further upstream. If there isn't, chances are the water is clean enough to drink. Once you have established this, only fill from a fast-flowing part of the stream, as stagnant pools may carry water that will upset your stomach. Finally, if you are really riding in the middle of nowhere and you are unsure of the water quality – even from drinking water taps at dwellings – carry water purification tablets. The water will taste a little chlorinated, but at least you know it is safe.

air – The amount of space between your tyres and the ground. The more, the better.

Allen key – A hexagonal tool used to loosen or tighten the majority of the bolts on a bike.

ATB – All-Terrain Biking or Bike. The same as MTB.

anchor bolt – The bolt that fixes brake and/or gear cables into place.

auger – To take samples of the local terrain, usually with your face, by crashing.

axle – The shaft around which wheels and cranksets rotate.

baby heads – Small round rocks on a trail, similar in size to their namesake but more difficult to ride over.

bail – To part company from your bike in anticipation of crashing.

barrel adjuster – Threaded attachment on brake or gear units that allows for fine adjusting.

BB – Bottom bracket, the bearing unit around which the crankset rotates.

berm – A banked corner.

bonk – To run out of energy.

BPM – Beats Per Minute – the measure of your heart rate.

brake boss – The mounting point for the brakes.

brake pad – The replaceable part of the brake that does the slowing down for you.

bunny hop – A skill that will help you clear small obstacles on the trail.

bushing – A sleeve used as a bearing on certain forks, pivots and jockey wheels.

cable – Braided wire used to operate brakes and gears.

cable housing – The sheath that guides the gear and brake cables.

chain – A series of links held together by pins; the life-blood of the drivetrain.

chain line – An imaginary line that connects the middle chainring and the middle rear sprocket.

chain ring – A toothed sprocket attached to a crankarm.

chain stay – The section of the frame that connects the BB and the rear dropouts.

chain suck – When the chain gets caught between the granny ring and the frame, often in muddy conditions and often when the chain and/or chainrings are worn.

chain whip – A tool used to remove sprockets.

clean – To make it through a technical section without dabbing.

clipless pedal – Pedals where the shoes engage via cleats, creating a firm bond that is released by twisting the heel outwards.

cog – Toothed sprocket on the rear hub.

compression damping – A setting to control the speed of absorption of the impact a bump makes on a shock's spring.

crank arm – The levers of a crankset that you turn with the pedals.

crank set – A unit comprising BB, crank arms and chainrings.

cross-country – The most common form of racing.

dab – To put a foot on the ground in a technical section.

damper – The unit in a shock that determines the rate of compression.

damping – The controlled absorption of the compression of a shock.

death cookies – Fist-size rocks on a trail that point you and your bike everywhere except where you are planning on going.

derailleur – The device that shifts the chain over sprockets or chainrings.

derailleur hanger – The part of the frame where the rear derailleur bolts on; usually replaceable due to its vulnerability.

dialed in – A perfectly set up bike.

disk brake – A motorcar-style braking system that has brakes working on disks attached to the hub, rather than the conventional rim brakes.

drivetrain – The chain, BB, cranks, chainrings, sprockets and derailleurs.

dropouts – The slots in the fork and chainstays where the wheels clamp in.

elastomer – Compressible synthetic material used in some suspension forks.

endo – To go over the bars of your bike.

epic – An extremely long ride. Preferably including mechanical and human drama.

face plant – The result of an endo or an auger.

fire road – a back road, just wide enough for emergency vehicles and plenty wide enough for bikers to ride two-abreast and chat.

flange – The raised portion of a hub that holds the spokes.

freewheel – The bit in the hub that purrs when you don't pedal.

granny gear – The lowest gear on the bike, the one your granny would need on all but the flattest roads, and you need on the steepest.

granny ring – The smallest chainring. See granny gear.

GripShift – Gear shifters that are part of the handlebar grip; change gear by twisting.

hammer – To ride hard.

hammer-head – A rider who only knows how to ride hard.

hardtail – A bike with front-only suspension.

headset – The bearing unit around which your steering rotates.

hydraulic brake – A powerful braking system, usually disk, that uses hydraulic oil instead of cables.

JRA – Just Riding Along; the preamble for virtually every rider-caused trip to the bike shop. Usually used when looking for a warranty replacement.

knobblies – Typical off-road tyres, with moulded tread for better grip.

line – The best route through any section of trail.

MTB – MounTain Biking or Bike.

nipple – The threaded nut that tightens spokes.

nose wheelie – The controlled action of riding along on your front wheel only. Uncontrolled, it is called an endo.

off-camber – Ground that slopes away from the direction of cornering.

pinch flat – A puncture caused by getting the tube caught between the rim and a rock.

preload – The setting that controls the amount of compression on a shock.

Presta valve – Also known as racing valve, the thinner and more user friendly tube valve available. See Schrader valve.

PSI – Pounds per Square Inch – the accepted unit of pressure when pumping up mountain bike tyres.

Rapidfire – Shimano's most successful shifting system.

rebound damping – The rate of return-to-normal a shock spring possesses.

rim – The outer ring of the wheel, to which the tyre is fitted.

roadie – A cyclist who has not yet embraced mountain biking.

saddle – The instrument of torture that connects our rear ends to the bike.

Schrader valve – Also known as car valve. See Presta valve.

singletrack – Nirvana for mountain bikers: a trail wide enough for just one bike.

skewer – The quick release mechanism that holds the wheels on.

snake bite – See pinch flat.

spider – The right crank arm without its chainrings.

spider patrol – The first rider to ride a trail in the morning, clearing cobwebs as he goes.

spoke – The tensioned wire that connects the rim to the hub, completing the wheel.

sprockets – The rear cogs.

standover – The amount of clearance between the top tube of the bike and your nether regions when you stop.

swingarm – The active part of a rear suspension unit.

switchback – A tight corner that covers almost 180 degrees.

tea party – When a group of riders stops and can't stop chatting when it is time to start riding again.

top tube – the almost-horizontal tube on the bike frame that seems designed to emasculate riders.

trackstand – Standing still on the bike without putting a foot down.

travel – the amount of suspension a bike or shock has.

V-brake – Rim brakes activated by pulling a cable.

washboard – Small, regular corrugations in the trail.

wash out – When one, or both wheels slide out from under you.

wheelbase – The distance between the front and rear axles.

wheelie – To ride on the back wheel only.

wild pigs – Badly adjusted brakes. They squeal when used.

Useful websites

ORGANIZATIONS

International Cycling Union (UCI)
The governing body of all forms of competitive cycling, and increasingly becoming involved in recreational cycling.
www.uci.ch

British Cycling Federation (BCF)
The national governing body in the United Kingdom.
www.britishcycling.org.uk

Australian Cycling Federation
The national governing body in Australia.
www.cycling.org.au

New Zealand Cycling
The national governing body in New Zealand.
www.bikenz.org.nz

USA Cycling
The national governing body in the USA.
www.usacycling.org

Cycling South Africa (CSA)
The national governing body in South Africa.
www.cyclingsa.com

International Mountain Biking Association (IMBA)
The grand-daddy of advocacy groups. US-based but with chapters in other countries too.
www.imba.com

EVENTS

The Cape Epic
Eight-day mountain bike race through the picturesque Southern Cape, at the foot of Africa. Billed as Africa's Magical and Untamed Race, and rightly so.
www.cape-epic.com

The Transalp Challenge
One of the original multi-day stage races, and the one that has remained in the fore-front of European riders' minds.
www.transalpchallenge.com

The Crocodile Trophy
1,400 km (868 miles) across the Aussie outback, in summer. Hot, dusty and only for the very dedicated.
www.crocodile-trophy.com

La Ruta de los Conquistadores
Three days of mud, mud and more mud in Costa Rica.
www.adventurerace.com

The TransRockies Challenge
Seven days in the Canadian rockies, riding with bears, salmon and other interesting people.
www.transrockies.com

Kona Sleepless in the Saddle
A 24 hour racing series in the United Kingdom.
www.konasits.co.uk

The 24 Hours of… Series
A 24 hour series in the USA. Home of the original all day race, Moab.
www.grannygear.com

OTHER ONLINE RESOURCES
www.mtnbikehalloffame.com
A peek into the history of the sport.

www.wombats.org
Women's Mountain Bike and Tea Society.

www.britishtrails.co.uk
A good general mountain biking site.

www.descent-world.co.uk
Downhill-oriented site.

www.mtbr.com
User-generated reviews of bikes and equipment.

www.mtbroutes.com
Mainly UK routes, but some US offerings and advice.

www.sheldonbrown.com
Just about anything you would ever want to know about bikes.

www.weightweenies.com
For when you need to know which make of brake cable will be lighter.

MAGAZINES AND MEDIA
www.bicycling.co.za
Bicycling South Africa magazine website

www.mbuk.com
Mountain Biking UK magazine website

www.mountainbike.com
Bicycling magazine website

www.bicyclingaustralia.com
Bicycling Australia magazine website

www.velonews.com
VeloNews magazine website

www.cyclingnews.com
Cyclingnews website

www.dirtragmag.com
Mountain bike forum

www.bike-magazin.de
Bike magazine website

PHOTOGRAPHIC CREDITS

All images courtesy of Steven Seaton and Mike King with the exception of the photographs listed below. Copyright rests with the photographers and/or their agents.

Key to locations: t = top; b = bottom; l = left; r = right; c = centre
(No abbreviation is given for pages with a single image, or pages on which all photographs are by the same photographer.)

CA = Cannondale bikes
GI = Giant bikes
GWP = Geoff Waugh Photos
KO = Kona bikes
MBUK = Mountain Biking UK

NHP = New Holland Publishers
SBP = Steve Bardens Photography
SCG = Saris Cycling Group
SP = Specialized bikes
SRM = Schoberer Rad Messtechnik

1 ....SBP	41 r ....GWP	115 t ......SBP	159 ....SBP
4 ....SBP	44 ....SBP	115 b ......GWP	162 t ......GWP
6 l & r ......SBP	46 ....SBP	116 ....SBP	162 b ......SBP
7 r ....SBP	50 ....SBP	117 ....SBP	163 ....SBP
11 ....GWP	52 ....SBP	118 ....SBP	164 b ......SBP
14 ....SBP	53 t ....SBP	119 ....SBP	166 ....SBP
15 ....SBP	54 ....SBP	120 ....SBP	167 t ......SBP
16 ....SBP	56 l ....SBP	121 ....SBP	167 b ......GWP
17 ....SBP	60 ....SBP	122 t ......GWP	168 t ......GWP
18 ....GWP	66 l ....GWP	122 b ......SBP	168 b ......SBP
19 ....GWP	66 r ....SBP	123 ....GWP	169 ....SBP
22 ....GWP	68 ....SBP	124 ....SBP	171 ....NHP
23 t ....GWP	69 b ....SBP	125 ....SBP	172 t ......NHP
23 b ....SBP	92 ....MBUK	133 ....SBP	173 ....NHP
25 ....GWP	93 ....MBUK	134 b ......SCG	174 ....NHP
28–29 ......SP	100 ....SBP	135 ....SRM	175 t ......NHP
30–31 ......GI	101 l ......SBP	143 ....SBP	175 b ......GWP
32 ....GI	105 ....SBP	144 ....SBP	176 ....NHP
33 b ....SBP	106 ....SBP	147 r ......SBP	177 ....NHP
34 b ....SP	107 ....SBP	148 ....SBP	179 t ......NHP
36 ....KO	108 ....SBP	149 ....SBP	179 b ......SBP
37 l ....GWP	109 ....SBP	150 r ......SBP	180 ....NHP
37 r ....SBP	110 ....SBP	152 t ......SBP	182 ....GWP
38 ....CA	111 ....SBP	152 b ......GWP	183 b ......GWP
39 ....KO	112 ....SBP	154 ....GWP	
41 l ....SBP	113 ....SBP	155 ....GWP	
41 c ....SBP	114 ....SBP	158 ....SBP	